Writing Advice For Teens

Creating Stories

By

Mike Kalmbach

OTHER BOOKS BY MIKE KALMBACH

Fiction:

The Caldarian Conflict

Into the Land of Iowah
(Expected February 2013)

Non-Fiction:

Writing Advice for Teens: Creating Stories

Writing Advice for Teens: Editing
(Expected October 2012)

Coming soon:

Writing Advice for Teens: Joining the Writing Community

Writing Advice for Teens: Preparing for Publishing

Writing Advice for Teens: Writing as a Career

Writing Advice for Teens: Writing Prompts

ACKNOWLEDGMENTS

In today's world, one cannot write in a vacuum. This book would not have been written half as well without the help of other talented writers and readers.

My parents, Roger and Barbara Kalmbach, always encouraged me to keep pushing boundaries and see what's beyond that next door (or window, or wall). Thanks for giving me a needed gentle push when needed.

Continued heartfelt gratitude goes to my critique partners: Ann Noser, Christa Worrell, and Danielle Allen Without the help of these talented ladies, this book would never have seen the light of day.

Many thanks to Alison Kemper for her candid feedback and helpful tips as I developed this book.

Special recognition goes to my beta readers: Amber Godfrey, Jon Gullixson, Babs Larson, Rose Hamlin, David Fingerman, and many of those already mentioned. You helped me ensure that my advice remained clear and succinct.

Without the support of my wife, I could not have spent the many long hours it takes to craft a work of this size. Brenda is an amazing woman, and this is my thanks.

And Alexander: you're still the reason I write.

Mike Kalmbach

BLANK PAGES ARE STORIES
BEGGING TO BE HEARD

TABLE OF CONTENTS

Other Books by Mike Kalmbach 4

Acknowledgments.. 5

Introduction 11

Goals of this book 11

Targeted for teens... 11

Who wrote this book? 12

You can make it as a writer....................................... 13

How to use this book... 15

Getting started 17

The writing mentality 18

Overcoming doubt... 20

What should I write? 22

Practical writing 24

Considerations for children's books (ages 3-7)........... 24

Considerations for writing fiction 25

Methods for writing humor 26

Take your writing seriously..................................... 28

Develop a writing routine.................................... 31

Keep a writer's journal 32

Grow as a writer.. 35

How to write 2000 words a day............................. 37

It's okay to take an occasional break...................... 42

Setting Goals 43

Identify long-term goals 43

Setting monthly goals.. 44

Track your progress.. 57

What tools should I use? 60

Scrivener 61

LitLift — A Free Novel-Writing Assistant 61

Write or Die! 62

Grindstone 62

Strategies for generating ideas **63**

Mystery door 63

Secrets in the attic 66

One-sentence prompts 67

Prompt Matrix 69

History prompts 70

Current events 73

Still life 75

Unusual uses for everyday objects 77

Diseases 79

Story construction **83**

Core concepts 83

Meet your characters 84

Perspective—who's telling the story 92

Setting—where it all happens 95

Basic plot structure 102

Develop a plan (outline) 115

Why outline? 115

Don't some authors just wing it? 115

Do I have to follow my outline? 118

What if I don't know the ending yet? 118

Why is the ending important? 119

Typical writing problems **121**

Writer's block 121

The perfect time to write 125

I had a great idea, but… 126

Help! My computer crashed!............................128

Crap, I have nothing to do!............................130

My teacher says I'm breaking the rules......................133

I've never taken drugs, but I want to write about someone who does......................135

FAQs..**139**

How do I get started writing?......................139

I have a cool book idea. Should I find a publisher? 139

What's the difference between writing and publishing? 140

How do I deal with writer's block?............................140

How do I become a better writer? 140

Which other writing books should I read? 141

How long should my story be?..................................141

How do I make my story longer? 141

How do I choose names for my characters, creatures, or settings?..142

How do I choose a point of view?..............................144

Is it okay to mix perspectives? 145

How do I make my dialogue sound realistic? 146

How do I know when my story is finished?................147

How should I handle criticism?..................................149

I just discovered a book/game/movie with the same plot. What should I do?...151

What about fan fiction?..152

How do I make my story unique? 152

What if someone tries to steal my idea?......................153

Parting Thoughts..**155**

Appendix A: Word Count Guidelines **157**

Appendix B: Example Character Sheet 159

Glossary 163

References.. 169

Index... 171

Picture Credits 174

Did you enjoy this book? 175

About the Author 176

INTRODUCTION

"If you want to write, write it. That's the first rule."

—Robert Parker

Goals of this book

Many new writers have trouble getting started. It's often tough to begin when all you have is a blank page.

This book aims to help you overcome that initial hurdle by making it easy for you to write down simple, focused ideas and craft them into stories.

After following the advice and using the techniques outlined in this book, you should understand how to bring the stories locked in your mind to the surface.

This advice goes beyond mere brainstorming. Sure, I'll show you some techniques to help focus your creative energies. And brainstorming is the typical method used for coming up with story ideas.

However, real writers do more than come up with ideas. Real writers understand how to separate the good ideas from the bad. Real writers know how to turn concepts into a story readers can't put down. I'll help you sketch strong skeletons that you can flesh out into full-fledged stories.

By the end of this book, you'll be well on your way to building unforgettable tales.

Targeted for teens

As a former teenager, I understand how hard it is to get helpful feedback on your stories from teachers, parents and friends. As writers, we want to know about weaknesses in our work so we can fix problems before our readers find them.

Unfortunately, most people don't know how to give constructive feedback. Often you'll receive comments like:

- "This is wonderful! I can't wait to read more."
- "I found a couple typos, but other than that it looks good!"
- "For someone your age, you have a lot of talent."

The biggest problem?

Your teachers, friends, and family all know you. They care about you. They don't want to hurt your feelings. They want you to succeed. And those are all good things.

Even so, most people don't understand that writers need solid, constructive critiques to take a story to the next level. One of the best ways to improve your skills is to join a critique group (more on that later).

That said, you can still learn some techniques to improve your writing through books. This book will help you understand how stories are formed. With a little structure and an understanding of what makes a story work, you'll soon learn how to create stories people want to read.

Who wrote this book?

As it says on the cover, my name is Mike Kalmbach. Over the past decade, I've mentored new writers both online and in the real world. For the past few years, I've moonlighted as a freelance editor, helping authors on the path to both traditional and self-publishing. I also lead the Rochester Minnesota Writing Group (more than 75 members and growing), founded the Rochester Writers Collaborative, and created a free online writing community called WritAnon, available at http://forum.writanon.com.

From my experiences working with writers of all skill levels, I've learned several strategies to help budding writers create better stories. Through seminars, I've already taught hundreds of students how to become better storytellers. This book provides a condensed resource that will guide you on your own personal writing journey.

You can make it as a writer

Age doesn't matter. I've seen amazing stories created by writers both young and old. The quality of the story is a result of the time and passion you put into it. Be passionate, and you will be great.

As a writer, someone will eventually say something to discourage you. Perhaps it will sound something like this:

- "Writing? What a waste of time!"
- "It's impossible to get published."
- "When are you going to stop dreaming and get a real job?"

Don't listen.

I spent about six years developing skills for a "real" job. I enjoyed (and still enjoy) programming computers. Still, one of my biggest regrets is that I stopped writing for those six years.

Stopping was a mistake.

Don't get me wrong: there is value to pursuing a career in any skill that catches your interest.

My mistake was assuming that I had to quit writing to pursue a full-time job. I could have done both.

> **Don't *just* write, but don't *just* pursue a career either.**
>
> **Do both.**

You will likely need a traditional job to survive in today's world. Still, keep writing something every day, even if it's just a hundred words. Every word gets you a little closer to your writing goals.

Writing doesn't require raw talent (although it helps). As you practice writing, you will improve. Hard work will win over raw talent every time. If you're curious about how this works, read *The Tipping Point* by Malcolm Gladwell.

Writing does require practice, patience, and constructive feedback. It also requires that you're well-read. The more books you've read, the better your own stories will likely be. You'll develop an intuitive sense for what makes a story entertaining.

Truly enjoyable stories come from the combination of life experiences with tons of writing practice. Real-life experiences give you raw material for stories.

In high school, you should take courses in journalism, English, creative writing, and history.

Why history? Knowing how events occurred in the past is a good way to guess how they might happen in the future.

In college, even if you're certain you want to be a writer, I'd recommend studying something outside just writing. Consider focusing on an interest area like computers, medicine, business, or teaching. Writers come from all backgrounds, and interest areas will give you more experience that you can draw on to improve your stories. Plus, if you're interested in a topic, your passion will come across in your writing.

For example, you might study software so you can create video games. Later on, you can potentially write a science fiction novel that's more realistic because you already understand how the technology works.

Focus on career: As it turns out, one of my editing clients originally created video games before working on his first novel. He recently scored a three-book deal with Del Rey, an imprint of Random House, which is one of the "Big Six" publishers.

After completing a Bachelor's degree, you might take courses toward a Master in Fine Arts (MFA) degree. Like other Master degree programs, an MFA usually requires that you have a Bachelor's degree. Unlike other Master degree programs, an MFA does not require a specific major (though you usually have to have a certain number of English credits to qualify for admission).

Do you need to earn a degree in the arts to be a writer? No. However, education gives you more tools that improve your chances of success. The better you understand the world, the more likely it is that you'll create stories that people want to read.

Very few people make a living just writing. On the other hand, the tide is changing. Recent advances with the "eBook revolution" have made it possible for more writers to earn a steady income. As you release additional projects, the chances increase that A) someone will find your work, and B) enough people will buy your work so you can live off the income.

The most financially successful writers have written dozens of books. You're not likely to make it big with just one book, but by having multiple high-quality books, you stand a decent chance at seeing financial success.

You can learn more about making money as a writer in another book in this series: *Writing Advice for Teens: Writing as a Career.*

How to use this book

This book consists of five different sections with separate goals. They can be read in any order, or you can cherry pick the aspects that most interest you.

- *Getting started:* General advice for any beginning writer. You'll find methods for helping you start writing like a professional.

- *Strategies for generating ideas:* How to overcome the sometimes-daunting blank page. Learn how to create story ideas from scratch.

- *Story construction:* Basic story structure to help you frame your ideas and develop an outline.

- *Typical writing problems:* Showcases common writing problems and how to recognize and resolve them.

- *FAQs:* Questions asked by virtually every beginning writer. The answers will help you avoid common mistakes and develop realistic expectations.

READY, SET, WRITE!

GETTING STARTED

*"An object at rest, stays at rest, and
an object in motion, stays in motion,
unless acted upon by an outside force."*
– Sir Isaac Newton, First Law of Motion

The blank page is the biggest challenge that a writer faces.

In everyday conversation, you usually don't think about each individual word you say. Instead, you think about the idea you want to convey, and the words fall out naturally.

For a first draft, capture that same energy. Don't think about the wording for every sentence. Nothing has to be perfect—polishing comes later, during the editing phase. For now, focus on recording the *ideas*, not the *wording*. Worry only about getting down the events you want to cover.

That leads us to our first exercise.

Exercise: Why write?

Why do you want to write? Are you looking to make money? Become famous? Share your stories with the world?

List all the reasons you like to write. Don't worry about complete sentences or perfect grammar. Just write them down for now. You can format them later.

Afterward:

Revise and post your reasons in your writing area. When you get stuck, remind yourself why you write. This is often enough to help you get moving again. Update your list whenever you find another reason to write.

---

really struggling with a section, ask yourself if it's really necessary, or if there's another way to incorporate the idea into your story. The reason you're struggling might be that the piece simply doesn't fit. Your subconscious may be telling you that you're making a mistake. Try removing the section to see how it works.

What should I write?

Every type of writing has its own quirks. Whether you're writing poetry, short stories, articles, or novels you'll face different challenges as you create new work.

Deciding what to write is a mix of where your skills and interests meet. Do you enjoy working with young children? You might write a story that teaches kids how to count or about the importance of looking both ways before crossing the street.

Do you want to create fascinating worlds? Science fiction or fantasy is probably for you. You'll have opportunities to invent any world you desire.

Can't resist romance? Then don't! Write about a relationship you'd love to experience.

In any case, pick something you like. You're probably going to spend more time than you realize with each piece of work, so you should enjoy it.

> **Write what you enjoy.**

I write for myself first, and others second. In my opinion, that's the best way to tell an effective story. Always pleasing others is impossible, but at least I have a shot at satisfying myself with something I write.

Why is this important?

My first publishable novel took about fifteen months to complete: nine months of writing the first draft (averaging about 300 words per day), and another six months performing multiple rounds of editing. Even though it was a lot of work, I enjoyed every minute I spent on it.

Likewise, you'll be spending a lot of time on your own projects. If you see writing as a joy, you won't mind investing the time every day to keep moving forward on your projects. Don't waste time on a project you don't enjoy.

If you're not sure what you'd like to write, but feel driven to write *something*, think about the stories you enjoy reading. For example:

- *Enjoy paranormal romance?* Consider writing a love story about a ghost who falls in love with the girl who moves into his haunted house.
- *Enjoy mysteries?* Consider writing a story about a student who stumbles across a teacher's dark secret.
- *Enjoy science fiction?* Consider creating a society that grows technology using plant life instead of building it with metals.

The possibilities are endless. Write for yourself first, and you'll soon find that others will enjoy your stories as much as you do.

Don't hesitate to include your experiences playing on a sports team or other extracurricular activities. If you have a hobby you enjoy, include it as a hobby for one of your characters. It could add another level of realism to your story.

Exercise: What do you enjoy?

Take five minutes and write down a list of things you enjoy. These can be books you've read, activities (riding horses, playing a sport, etc.), and feelings you experience (like your stomach dropping when riding a roller coaster).

Afterward:

Review your list. Can you turn these things into stories? What would happen if you couldn't do one of those things anymore? How would that make you feel?

Practical writing

It's possible to get valuable writing experience even while you're in high school. Most schools offer courses in college writing and activities like yearbook or a school newspaper. Ask your counselor or English teacher about opportunities in your school.

Most libraries have newsletters. Ask your local library if they'd accept a submission from a student for their newsletter. It's a good way to build up writing samples (also known as "clips") that you can use later in your writing career.

Considerations for children's books (ages 3-7)

Writing for children may result in shorter stories, but you need to be careful of the words you choose. For example, even a common word like "challenges" may be beyond the skill of the children reading the story.

Also, like poetry, each word must count. Keep the story moving forward, or you'll bore your readers.

There's a lot of debate about whether children's books should rhyme, so write whatever you're most comfortable with. In any case, children's books tend to fall into one or more of the following categories:

- Teach a skill (identifying colors, counting, etc.)
- Demonstrate a moral or social value (being honest even if it's hard, loving your family, etc.)
- Show cause and effect (how "crying wolf" can mean that people won't help you when you need it, etc.)
- Explain something about how the world works (animals, cars, etc.)
- Reveal history and culture (biographies, holidays, etc.)
- Show how language works (poetry, songs, etc.)

You'll also often see the "rule of three" used in children's books. Each time, the pattern gets a slight twist. This helps kids see patterns and how to learn from past experiences.

For example, one children's book might use the following sequence of events to show how plants grow:

1) A child plants three seeds in separate cups. Two are set in a window that gets plenty of sun, and the other is placed in a dark basement. Two of the plants get water: the one in the basement and one of those in the window.

2) A few days later, the child checks on the plants. Two have sprouted: the plants that got water. The two surviving plants receive more water.

3) A few days later, the child checks the plants again. The one in the window has grown healthy and strong. The one in the basement has withered and died.

The lesson, of course, is that plants require both light and water to live. The journey of discovery is what teaches a child about the world. You can find out more about the rule of three in *Writing Advice for Teens: Editing*.

Considerations for writing fiction

Fiction allows us to share stories crafted from our imagination. We can throw characters into any situation and watch how they handle events. In some ways, it's like being in control of your own private world.

There are often many paths a story could take, and even if you know the beginning, some of the events in the middle, and the end, you don't really know how the story is going to look until you write it. By the end, each character's decisions form the world that surrounds them.

> **Writing is a creative process. It's okay to make mistakes.**

Stories require three things:

- A plot with a compelling conflict
- Characters who are interesting and feel like they could be real people
- A setting where it all happens

Balancing the three aspects is what all storytellers practice. Most writers are strong in at least one aspect, but to write captivating stories, you need to develop strengths in all three.

You can learn more about crafting stories in the section labeled *Story Construction* later in this book.

Methods for writing humor

Humor is one of the toughest things to translate into writing.

To be fair, writers are hamstrung: we can't use intonation, hand gestures, or other visual/audial cues to help convey that we're joking.

We only have words. Yet, there are some writers who are able to make us laugh seemingly without effort. How do they do it?

Method 1: Yes, and...

In improv acting, one of the basic techniques that actors use is to never say "no". Denying what someone else has said or done is rarely funny. For example, read this "joke" pickup line.

```
Man: "Haven't I seen you somewhere before?"

Woman: "No."
```

Not very funny, right?

On the other hand, accepting a statement and taking it in a new direction can be hilarious. This is often used in more successful pickup line jokes.

```
Man: "Haven't I seen you somewhere before?"

Woman: "Yes. That's why I don't go there
anymore."
```

Method 2: Surprise twist

One of the most common methods for a joke is to offer a twist that sends your reader down one path and switches direction at the last moment. Consider this poem (written by yours truly):

```
Today I ran, first time in a while,
At first it does hurt, but I know it's worthwhile,
I jump over logs, show my own unique style.

Pain is caused by weeks (months) of neglect,
Push through it, I must, to improve the effect
For retaining my health, which I must protect.

More bushes appear, I bound right on through,
Legs pumping, arms swinging on cue,
I run, though I know not where to.

Sweat pours down my face, my neck, and my back,
Though tired, found strength I feared that I lack.
What motivation when a bear wants you as a snack!
```

On a second read through, the poem takes on a completely different meaning, doesn't it?

Method 3: Multiple meanings

This method relies heavily on the language being used, and in this case, the ambiguity of the English language. The hardest to translate into other languages, this technique can upset your reader's expectations through careful use of emphasis.

```
    "I was walking down the street
yesterday, and I saw a jogger. She was
smokin'."

    "Pretty hot, eh?"

    "No. She stopped, pulled out a
cigarette, and lit it up. Couldn't believe
my eyes!"
```

Using these techniques can help you turn solemn dialogue into a vibrant conversation.

> **Exercise:** Tell a joke
>
> Think about an event that happened earlier today. Could it have happened differently? Try one of the three methods and see how it works.
>
> **Afterward:**
>
> Did your joke make you laugh? It's okay if it didn't. It takes practice to write good humor.
>
> Over the next day, watch how people interact. When you hear someone answer a question with the word "no", think about whether there's a way to turn it into a "yes." If you work at humor, you can soon be writing jokes that make everyone laugh.

Take your writing seriously

Writing should be treated—but not dreaded—like homework. It needs to be done every day, and projects should have a due date.

The best way to improve consists of two steps:

1) Write every day. Set word count goals and meet them.
2) Surround yourself with writers you respect.

Like practicing for a sport or academic event, writing requires dedication. The biggest challenge is showing up to write your 500, 1000, or even 2000 words every day.

Too busy? Take ten minutes to write every day. Even the busiest people can find ten minutes a day to make some progress.

Start out at an easy pace. Write just 100 words every day for a week, then increase your goal as this becomes easier.

What does 100 words look like? This three-paragraph example consists of exactly 100 words. When you see it lain out like this, it's not quite so intimidating.

In most cases, you can pound out 100 words in about five to ten minutes. Take advantage of short breaks, such as waiting for a bus or the moments before a meal. Fit in a couple minutes after you get up or before you go to bed.

Three short paragraphs; that's all it takes to be 100 words closer to achieving your goals. Small steps will help you to finish your manuscript quickly.

Writers should always strive to improve themselves and their craft. Each week, examine how your writing went.

- Did I reach my word count goals every day? If not, why?
- What were my barriers to writing? Examples: social media, playing games, etc.
- How much time did I spend writing? Did I stay focused, or was I distracted?
- Can I write even more next week? Should I increase my word count goal?
- Could I have made the story simpler? Could I have figured this out before I wrote?
- Do the actions of my characters make sense in their world? Will my reader understand them?

By asking yourself these questions, you keep yourself accountable and find more productive ways to spend your time. There's nothing wrong with playing games or interacting on social media, but if it's interfering with your writing (or other parts of your life), consider cutting back. Alternatively, you can use social media or games as a reward for accomplishing your writing goals each day.

To find writers you respect, I'd recommend joining a writing group that you submit writing samples to regularly.

Getting consistent feedback on what you do well and where you can improve helps you develop as a writer.

I belong to several writing communities, both online and in the real world. Each is helpful for different reasons. Find out more in *Writing Advice for Teens: Joining the Writing Community*.

Feedback is a writer's fuel; it helps us grow. Even so, make sure that your work is grammatically ready to review before you have others read it.

To get the best feedback, polish your work before you submit it. There should be no obvious typos or grammar errors, and you should feel like the submission is as good as you can make it on your own. This means reviewing your work multiple times before handing it in for others to critique. This allows your reviewers to focus on content, not grammar.

Sometimes, especially for longer works, you may want to submit a piece that isn't finished yet. For example lengths, I use the following guidelines when submitting to my writing groups:

- Short stories – complete and self-revised
- Novellas – at least 25% complete
- Novels – outlined and at least 20% complete

Even though you may have much of your story complete, you probably won't submit all of it to a writing group at once. Out of respect for each other's time, most writing groups set a word or page count limit, such as 3000 words or 10 pages per meeting.

You can find out more about suggestions for running a writing group in *Writing Advice for Teens: Joining the Writing Community*.

Why follow these guidelines?

It shows respect to your reviewers. People become frustrated by reading sloppy work. If you're going to use friends or teachers, keep in mind that they're using their free time to read your work, so use their time as efficiently as possible. This shows how much you respect their feedback.

Develop a writing routine

One of the hardest aspects of writing, as with any other habit, is committing to writing every day, even if just for fifteen minutes.

Developing a writing routine is kind of like brushing your teeth. Once you've gotten in the habit, it's relatively painless to do every day. On the other hand, if you skip a day or two, it's easier to stop.

Writing every day helps you get past this problem. I spend at least 15-30 minutes writing every day, even when I'm at my busiest.

When creating your writing routine, start with the following guidelines:

- **Close the door.** This shuts out the world and allows you to focus on your writing.
- **Turn off all distractions.** If you can't work in complete silence, consider using a white noise maker like a fan, songs written in a language you don't understand, or instrumental music. This leaves the language processing portions of your brain free to focus on your writing.
- **Disconnect from the Internet.** This removes the temptation to check social networks or email.
- **Clear your desk or table of any non-writing essentials.** This removes the temptation to fiddle with knickknacks instead of writing.
- **If using a computer, shut down all applications except for your word processor.** Again, this allows you to focus. It's even better if you use the full-screen option provided by most word processors.
- **Write at the same time every day.** Similar to brushing your teeth every morning and night, writing at the same time and place will help you turn this practice into a routine.

Each writer will ultimately create his or her own routine. Some like to write on the bus or train during a commute. Others like to work at the library, or over their lunch hour.

Whatever you choose, just do it consistently. There are no wrong answers here, but these guidelines seem to work for most people.

Another part of my writing routine includes working on different emotions and styles. If I want to write something cheerful, I first read several cheerful stories, listen to cheerful music, or watch a funny movie. That helps get me in the right state of mind to write something happy. This also works for other moods and styles (scary movies to write horror, etc.).

It's better to set a small goal and beat it than to set a big goal and miss it. For example, if you set a goal of 200 words a day and end up writing 300, you will feel pretty good. If you set a goal of 400 words a day and only write 300, you'll feel bad about missing your goal. If you're consistently hitting 300 words a day, then it's fine to raise your goal.

The important part is to get started. Today, not tomorrow.

Keep a writer's journal

One of the best ways to monitor your progress as a writer is to maintain a journal.

A writer's journal allows you to keep track of the days you're successful, the things that inspire you, techniques or strategies you learn, and how many words you can complete each day. This holds you accountable—when you know that you have to record your progress each day, you're more likely to meet your goals.

Here are a few things you should consider recording every day. Try to spend less than five minutes on each entry.

- The number of words you wrote and how much time you spent writing
- A quick summary of any articles/chapters that you wrote
- Anything that inspired you while writing today (movies, something a friend said, a memory, etc.)
- Techniques you used to generate ideas (brainstorming, using an outline, speaking out loud, etc.)

- Any publishing credits you've earned—for example, publishing an article in your school newspaper or winning a writing contest
- Classes taken and/or interesting articles you've read. Include how to find them again, such as recording the web address or publication
- Distractions that occurred while you were writing (people or pets interrupting, music or television shows going on in the background, whether you visited websites as you were working, etc.)
- Important feedback you received from teachers, friends, or other writers.

Here's an example from my own writing journal:

Date: 11/17/2011

Words written today: 592

Notes: Worked on Chapter 4 for Into the Land of Iowah. Researched magic stores in Ames, Iowa, and discovered that there actually is one that I could use.

Inspirations: Discovered interesting connections between card games and "real" wizardry.

Notice how this entry is short. I include just enough detail to jar my memory at a later time.

Keeping track of these items will help you to understand how you're improving as a writer. Looking back at these journal entries will help you see how far you've come, as well as how to make yourself more productive as a writer.

Looking at your best days will help you figure out what factors contributed to your success. After you've recorded your progress every day for a month, look for some common factors on the days where you performed well and on the days where you didn't write as much.

For example, you may find some of the following correlations:

- On days that you were **most** successful, there were fewer distractions (no interruptions, no checking email, etc.)
- On days that you were **least** successful, you were watching a movie at the same time as you wrote
- Rewards for a certain amount of progress resulted in achieving your goal
- Watching specific movies, listening to music, or reading certain books before writing tended to inspire you

Try using a writer's journal for a month, and see what you learn. I've found it to be a valuable tool for monitoring my own progress, keeping track of what I learn, and improving as a writer.

Exercise: Journal entry

Get a new notebook. Take five minutes and record what you've done today for your own writing. Answer some of the questions above, but stop writing after five minutes. You should never spend more time on your journal than you do on your "real" writing.

Afterward:

Place your notebook somewhere you will see it every day. Write an entry in your writing journal talking about your writing every day.

Grow as a writer

Books aren't written in one sitting. They're written one page at a time.

When you start your own projects, keep them small and measurable. It's easier to begin with short stories. After you've gained some experience with those, take what you've learned (what you liked, what you didn't like) and combine some of those ideas into a larger story.

After you've finished and polished a few short stories, get some feedback from people you trust. Ideally, this will be someone who will both encourage you and give useful ideas for improvement.

Be aware that friends and family may not point out every flaw because they'll often try to be considerate of your feelings. If you've joined a writing group, this would be a perfect place to try that first submission. Writers understand what feedback you desire.

As you grow in skill, you'll be better able to write longer works. This is a result of your growing focus and experience.

> **Maintain focus. Avoid writing with distractions.**

Even though most of us hate to admit it, humans are poor at managing multiple things at once. Focus on just one project at a time. With each additional project, it's harder to see progress and harder to ensure that you're getting things done.

Experiments have shown that people are more productive in a distraction-free environment. I've even performed my own tests to see how productive I am both with and without distractions. I highly recommend that you do so also. The results opened my eyes to the importance of focusing on my work.

Here's the experiment:

For one of my novels, my writing goal was to write around 500 words each day. I decided to measure how much time I spent each night writing, and how many words I was able to generate. For the next three weeks, I tried varying the amount of distraction in my writing routine.

For my first week, I used my normal routine: writing while a movie or some music played in the background. I found it took around 2-2.5 hours to write my 500 word quota, often taking breaks to watch the movie or sing along with a song.

During the second week, I turned off all distractions, including my Internet connection and my phone. I wrote more (averaging about 750 words) and spent much less time: 1-1.5 hours. This left me with time to really enjoy a movie or get some sleep.

While I wasn't exactly surprised that I was more productive with silence, I was a little surprised at the amount of difference–150% more output in about half the time.

I also found one additional productivity boost in the third week: listening to music I find inspiring immediately before I started work. This boosted my average to around 800 words in the 1-1.5 hour time frame.

While revising my novel several weeks later, I discovered another benefit. The sections I'd written while having fewer distractions had fewer errors and required less editing. Not only was I writing a lot more in less time, but the quality was significantly better.

For me, the results were clear: writing with fewer distractions saves a ton of time.

Exercise: My distractions

Take a piece of paper and divide it into two columns. Take a few minutes to write down all the distractions you might encounter on the left side. On the right side, write down what you can do to avoid that distraction.

Examples:

The Internet	Disable my connection
Text messages	Turn off my phone
Siblings	Shut my bedroom door

Afterward:

Post your list in your writing area. If a distraction occurs, act on your response. Once you're done writing for the day, you can deal with distractions.

Note: This may also help you focus on homework.

Consider sharing your list with your parents. They may even be able to help you come up with even better ways to respond to distractions.

How to write 2000 words a day

This isn't something you want to attempt right away. Wait until you have some experience, or this could end up frustrating you.

Feel free to change the number to something that's realistic for you. If that number is 100 words, these tips still work. This should be a fun challenge, not a dreaded exercise.

While finishing the first draft of a recent novel, I tried to write 2000 words or more each day. In order to write that much every day, I had to change my habits. I also found that while this was okay for a few weeks, I couldn't sustain it for more than a month. However, consider this: at 2000 words per day, you only need a month (or maybe a little more) to finish a first draft of a 60,000-word novel.

A few things helped me succeed, so I want to share those tips with you.

Tip 1: Turn off the Internet, TV, and phone

I know I covered this earlier, but seriously, you have to turn it off. In the age of Twitter, blogging, constant bombardment from news, etc., there are too many distractions to keep you from focusing on writing.

As I mentioned before, I used to write while playing a movie for "background noise", but often found myself distracted by whatever was on. Another bad habit I had was checking email or Twitter every five or ten minutes.

Note: When I say turn off the Internet, I really mean just your wireless connection. Please don't unplug your house's Internet connection. Your family might get a little angry, to say the least.

Eventually, I decided to simply disconnect the Internet while writing and made a conscious decision to leave it off. Now I'm able to focus on writing instead of checking my email.

Tip 2: Don't sit down to write 2000 words at once

I've found a lot more success when I focus on writing a scene or a much smaller goal, like 100 words. I can write 100 words in 3-5 minutes. At that pace, it will take 1-2 hours to write 2000 words.

Blocking aside 1-2 hours seems hard, while breaking it into a few 30-minute chunks makes it a lot easier. With 30 minutes at lunch, 30 minutes before dinner, and 30 minutes before bed, there are one-and-a-half hours right there. I can usually find the extra time somewhere else (generally a little longer at night).

Tip 3: Focus on scenes, not word counts

Sometimes we get too focused on numbers. Word counts are only helpful if you're still making useful progress on your story every day. Writing fluff to make your word count isn't useful because you'll just have to cut it out later.

If you find yourself too focused on making your word count, try focusing on scenes instead.

Each of my scenes tends to run from 1000-3000 words. By focusing on completing a scene, I take the pressure off just filling out my word counts. As an added benefit, most of my scenes flow better because they were written at one time.

That being said, if I'm stuck, I'll fall back to just writing 100 words in a sitting. Small goals are easy to achieve. You may not be able to move a mountain, but given enough time, you could build a new one using a single pebble at a time.

More details on constructing scenes are available in a later chapter.

Tip 4: Don't edit

Don't revise your work at first. Turning off the internal filter is one of the big challenges writers face.

Editing comes later, once your first draft is ready. And there's plenty of work to do on your first draft before it's ready for editing.

I've already shown some examples where I've talked about my internal editor, or the voice that points out problems within a work in progress. As you gain skill, your internal editor will help you improve your own stories. At the same time, learn to ignore your internal editor until *after* you've finished your first draft. It's much easier to edit once you've got the full story down.

Tip 5: When you finish one section, outline the next

It's nearly impossible to keep an entire book in your mind at the same time. On the other hand, it's completely possible to hold one scene in focus.

I tend to sketch out the skeleton of the next scene when I've finished working on my current one. This helps me to maintain focus and understand my mindset the next time I sit down to write.

Your outline doesn't need to be extremely detailed. Here's one example of some notes I took for a scene from my debut novel, *The Caldarian Conflict*. It shows a scene I added specifically to introduce the main character, a monk named Mendell, as he found out that he would have to guide a pirate prisoner through his execution.

Scene beginning:

Candlelight flickered across Mendell's face. The paper crackled as he turned a page.

"Three men stood accused of similar crimes: each had been accused of stealing from a merchant.

"The first came forward to be judged."

(note: rest of scene is incomplete)

Goal:

Introduce Mendell, show that abbey is more than just infirmary

Mood:

Mendell is focused, then annoyed at being interrupted

Events:

o Studies a tome on justice, perhaps reading a short parable that summarizes the approach to justice in this world

- Three men accused of the same crime, but for different motives

- Crimes decrease in severity (revenge, feed others, hunger)

o Mention that followers of Lord Justice should be tempered by lessons from other gods/goddesses because of the fact that every situation is unique, and that no single punishment is appropriate

o Novice interrupts to say that Father Ramsey would like to speak to him

o Mendell talks briefly with Father Ramsey about being assigned to the execution (something about priests vs. monks)

As you can see, there is just enough detail to record my thoughts, without actually writing the story. Also note that since this was a note to me, I didn't have to explain every small detail. The next day, I sat down and fleshed out the full scene. Writing down a few thoughts at the end of a writing session helps focus you when you sit down again.

Tip 6: Find a writing buddy (or a group of them)

Each week, I submit my work to a group of like-minded writers who want to focus on increasing word counts without sacrificing quality. By critiquing each other's work, we also sharpen our skill by catching each other's errors.

One of the things I've noticed is that I now hear the other writer's voices in my head as I write. They'll encourage me to focus on bringing out a character quirk, or adding that extra little twist of detail. Each week, I find that my writing grows stronger.

To find a group, check at your local library to see if a young writers group already exists. If one does not, you may want to either join up with an adult writing group (assuming there is one), or start your own writing group at your school. If you're planning to start your own group, ask your English, journalism, or creative writing teachers if one of them would be interested in mentoring the group.

Find more tips on joining or creating a writers group in *Writing Advice for Teens: Joining the Writing Community.*

It's okay to take an occasional break

Life is hectic. Many times we feel pressured to have something going on every night and weekend. We push so hard that we find ourselves wondering how we're going to get it all done.

There's a reason why schools give occasional days off, and that adults get vacations from work. Once in a while, you simply need a break. The trick is to keep your breaks well-defined, and to know when to start writing again.

It's okay to take a day off from writing. However, since writing is a voluntary activity, avoid taking more than one day off at a time. It's much harder to get started again once you've stopped.

Sometimes a much shorter break is all you need. For example, you might get frustrated with a current project. Nothing seems to be coming together. The words just won't flow. Your conclusion doesn't make sense, even to you.

Then you decide to take a walk, and when you sit down again, suddenly your words flow together much more easily.

Have you ever had a brilliant idea while taking a shower?

There's actual brain science behind why that happens. Creative thought occurs in the cerebral cortex, but this region of the brain is only active when you're relaxed. When you're feeling stressed, the cerebral cortex actually shuts down while your body moves into "fight or flight" mode.

You can work while stressed, of course, but the results won't be as creative. If you're feeling frustrated, relax by taking a walk or singing a song. You might find that the answers come more easily because your brain is literally better able to create.

If you're interested in how creativity works in the brain, I recommend reading Roseanne Bane's research paper entitled *The Writer's Brain: What Neurology Tells Us about Teaching Creative Writing*.

Setting Goals

Taking time to think about where you want to take your writing career is a valuable task. Setting goals and **writing them down** is even more vital. Post them somewhere you'll notice often, and you'll be more likely to achieve them.

Each day, ask yourself what you've done today to help achieve them. If nothing, take five minutes to advance towards one of your goals. You'll be amazed by how much difference those five minutes can make. Five minutes a day is 150 minutes a month—or 2.5 hours. Even a small amount adds up quickly.

Identify long-term goals

Understanding long-term goals will help you focus on smaller tasks that get you there. Examples might be to:

- write a novel
- publish a short story in a magazine
- create a book of poetry or short stories

There are many other possibilities, of course. Once you know where you want to go, the next step is to break the big goal into smaller chunks.

Focus on one goal at a time. It's okay to have lots of ideas, but you'll work faster by putting all of your energy into one project. Also, you'll find that focusing your effort will help you avoid frustration and accomplish your goals more quickly.

Setting monthly goals

First, start small. Just like exercise, you need to build up your writing muscle before you can tackle larger challenges.

In most cases, writers lose steam because they try to achieve too much and get frustrated by the lack of progress. Breaking your big goals into more manageable chunks is a way to avoid tons of headaches and false starts. It also gives you more opportunities to identify issues and fix them before they become problems.

Make sure that each goal is SMART:

Specific:	What do I want to accomplish?
Measurable:	How do I know I achieved my goal?
Attainable:	Can I complete this goal on time?
Relevant:	Does this relate to my long-term goal?
Time-bound:	How much time do I have?

Below, I've outlined two example plans to help you

1) complete a first draft of a novel

2) publish a story in a magazine.

Don't feel like you have to follow each plan exactly, but instead use this as a starting point for your own custom plan. You might be able to write a lot more, or you may feel like the listed goals are still too big. Go ahead and move things around.

Please note: I always leave a couple days at the end of the month available for when something takes a bit longer than expected. That way I'm more likely to hit all of my goals each month. If I finish faster, then I start pulling in additional work from the next month.

Also, when you're planning out each month, consider how much time you'll have available. It's likely you'll be able to finish much more during summer months while you're on vacation from school. During the school year, you may want to plan less—especially when you know you'll have big exams.

As mentioned in earlier sections, writers must read. Build time into your schedule to read at least a couple of books a month (preferably more).

Both schedules start out in a similar manner. Read carefully for the differences.

Example 1: Writing a novel

Expected time to completion of first draft: 6-8 months

Month 1:

- **Days 1-10:**
  - Read *Writing Advice for Teens: Creating stories* (**Note:** you're doing this now!)
- **Days 10-12:**
  - Generate at least five story beginnings (if you're stuck, use the strategies in the next chapter)
- **Days 12-22:**
  - Read *20 Master Plots* by Ronald B. Tobias
- **Day 23:**
  - Pick one of the story beginnings that you'll want to expand
  - Pick one of the Master Plots and think about how your story would likely end
  - Determine three major events that will happen between your beginning and ending.
- **Days 24-25:**
  - Write a sample ending

Variations on this plan:

- If you include reading in your plan (and you should), you don't need to read each book in one sitting. You can read a few chapters, work on generating a beginning, and then read a few more chapters.
- You can write the ending first. Some people enjoy this approach.
- You can create more major events (emotional interactions, physical encounters, etc.). Three to five is pretty standard. Any more than that and the book tends to feel too long.

Here's a short example of what you might have by the end of Month 1. A big part of the reason there's so little here is that you will spend most of your month reading. This is an investment in your own writing skill that will pay off many times over as you write more material.

Your beginning and ending will probably be longer than this. A couple pages for each will usually be sufficient.

Story beginning:

"Ohmigod, ohmigod, ohmigod!" Ellie screeched as the tightrope swayed back and forth over a yawning chasm. "This is way too much work to go to the cafeteria."

"We just want to make sure you're really hungry," the wizard teacher called from the floating classroom. "That's what keeps you working on your spells."

Ellie finally took the last stumbling step and made it to the platform that held the cafeteria. She pushed open the door to discover her sworn enemy, Kathryn.

Master plot used as a model: Rivalry

Considerations:

With a rivalry, the two characters need to be able to compete against each other, usually with different but related skills. The major events in the story need to highlight the conflict between these characters.

There are a few ways that a rivalry can end:

- One rival can defeat the other
- Both rivals need to work together toward a common goal
- Both rivals eventually become friends through mutual respect

Since the two characters are female and my target audience would likely be teenage girls, I'm most interested in the third option, where the two characters eventually earn each other's respect through their conflict.

Major events I plan to include in my story:

- Ellie and Kathryn compete against each other for a top position in the wizard school. Kathryn receives higher marks after sabotaging Ellie's potion by swapping out a needed ingredient, perhaps something like salt for sugar (since they look the same).
- Ellie gets mad and wants to get even. She casts a spell or creates a potion that makes Kathryn, who is proud of her appearance, break out with tons of zits. Bonus points if they burst in class. (Yeah, I know: Ew!)
- The wizard teacher recognizes the rivalry and asks the two to work together in order to complete a project that will represent the entire school.

Ending:

    Kathryn extended her hand. "You know, I
    never thought I'd say this, but we worked
    well together."

    Ellie smiled. "Yeah. We really showed
    those snobs at Hawthorne a thing or two.
    Think Brandy will ever get the custard out
    of her hair?"

    Kathryn laughed. "Who cares? She
    deserved it. See you next year?"

    "Can't wait. Have a great summer!"

Is this a perfect story? Of course not. We're just getting started.

Even so, there are some hints of a promising tale—the two girls are in training at some wizard school, which immediately calls to mind images of *Harry Potter*. At the same time, it's pretty clear they're not at Hogwarts.

Beyond that, there's opportunity here because we can follow two young women as they compete against each other in a magical school where even going to the cafeteria is a challenge.

This sample is just long enough to show that the story has potential. The major events help flesh out the story a little more, giving us a better idea of where we want the story to go.

Why work on the ending right away?

If you understand where your story should end, you can introduce hints of upcoming events, or foreshadowing, in early scenes. Since I know they will eventually respect each other, I need to start giving them reasons to like each other right away (even if they're blinded by their rivalry). And I'll also want the reader to respect both Kathryn and Ellie so the ending remains satisfying.

Remember that you're free to change your beginning or ending at any time. If you come up with a better idea, you can always throw your original beginning or ending away and rewrite another version.

Month 2:

- **Days 1-10:**
    - Read *On Writing* by Stephen King (**Note:** Don't get confused. The first half is an autobiography, and most of the writing advice is in the second half).
- **Day 11:**
    - Determine the total word count you'd like to achieve. A good target for a young adult novel is between 60,000 and 80,000 words (see *Appendix A* for a more in-depth discussion of typical word counts).

- o Determine how many words you think you can write every day. To start, an achievable goal is 300 words per day. If you can write more, great!
- o Estimate how many days it will take you to finish if you work every day. Create a countdown calendar to keep you motivated.
- **Days 12-30:**
  - o Begin work on your story after completing the above steps. Aim for your target word count every day!

Variations on this plan:

- You don't have to write the story in the order it will be read. Even so, it's a good idea to connect the introduction to the first major event because you're still learning about the characters and their world. Once you better understand the characters and setting, you'll be better able to write sections out of order.
- If you read more quickly than indicated, shift tasks forward. Also, feel free to work on your own story on the same days you read a book. Do what works for you.

By the end of two months, you'll have a good start on your novel. If you write 300 words a day for the full 20 days, you'll have 6,000 words, or almost 10% of your novel complete. Of course, if you write more each day, you'll be even farther ahead. At 1,000 words per day, you'd already be at 20,000 words, or between 20% and 30% done!

> **Pro Tip:** While setting a target word count is important, this is just a goal. If your story is finished in 50,000 words, don't add fluff to stretch the story to 60,000. A target word count merely allows you to estimate how much work you have left.

Your goal this month is to connect your introduction with the first major event. You'll also be spending time introducing your characters and world, so it's an exciting time.

Months 3-8 (or until complete):

- **Days 1-10:**
    - Find a book similar to what you're writing (also known as a "comparable" novel) and read it. If you're writing a paranormal romance, find other highly rated paranormal romance books. If you're writing a mystery, read a mystery targeted for the same age group you're targeting.
- **Day 11:**
    - Reexamine how many words you think you can write every day. Increase your word count by at least 100 words over your Month 2 goal.
- **Every day:**
    - Continue work on your story every day. Aim for your target word count!

Keep in mind: it's always okay to schedule a couple days off each month.

When you're reading books by other authors, take notes on what you like and dislike. See if you can add similar concepts to your own story (without copying) to make your story better. Check out cliffhanger example earlier in this chapter if you're stuck.

At the same time, look for what you can do differently from the author you're reading. Watch for opportunities to make your own story stronger, but be careful to avoid mimicking the voice and style of the story you're reading. Your story should remain unique, with your own unique voice.

While you're writing your first draft, if you discover a scene you'd like to rewrite, just take a note for now and store it safely away in a place you won't forget (perhaps attached to your novel's outline). Your goal over these months is to finish your first draft, not to necessarily have a perfectly polished novel.

A first draft is rarely (if ever) ready to publish. Once you've finished, it's time to revise. Read *Writing Advice for Teens: Editing* for strategies to revise your novel.

Example 2: Publish short stories in magazines

Please note: For completeness, the full schedule is included here. It is similar to the other examples, so look carefully for the differences.

Expected time to first published story: 6-12 months, sometimes longer

Month 1:

- **Days 1-10:**
  - o Read *Writing Advice for Teens: Creating stories* (**Note:** you're doing this now!)
- **Days 10-12:**
  - o Generate at least five story beginnings (if you're stuck, use the strategies in the next chapter)
- **Days 13-22:**
  - o Read *20 Master Plots* by Ronald B. Tobias
- **Day 23:**
  - o Pick one of the story beginnings that you'll want to expand
  - o Pick one of the Master Plots and think about how your story would likely end
  - o Determine three major events that will happen between your beginning and ending
- **Days 24-27:**
  - o Write the short story for at least one of your story beginnings

Variations on this plan:

- You don't have to read books in one sitting. You can read a few chapters, work on generating a beginning, and then read a few more chapters.
- If you have more time, write a few short stories. Focus on your favorite one at first, making it as good as possible.

The second month is where you'll start to notice some big differences from Example 1. When submitting to magazines, you'll need to understand how to write a query or cover letter. These letters are used to propose stories to magazine editors so they can determine whether your story is a good fit.

Query and cover letters are a topic for another book, and *The Writer's Digest Guide to Query Letters* is an excellent reference for learning how to write these essential documents.

Month 2:

- **Days 1-10:**
  - Read *On Writing* by Stephen King (**Note:** Don't get confused: The first half is an autobiography, and most of the writing advice is in the second half).
- **Days 11-14:**
  - Write a new short story following a similar process to last month.
- **Days 15-20:**
  - Read *The Writer's Digest Guide to Query Letters*
- **Days 21-23:**
  - Pull out your short story from last month. Read through it and see if there are ways to improve the story. Edit it to make those improvements.
- **Days 24-27:**
  - Write a cover letter to a fictional editor that describes your story. Use *The Writer's Digest Guide to Query Letters* to decide how to improve your letter. Don't send it yet!

Variations on this plan:

- If you read more quickly than indicated, shift tasks forward. Also, if you are able, feel free to work on your own story on the same days you read a book.

At this point, after going through your first round of revisions, ask a couple of other writers to review your story.

Ask them for honest feedback on the following items:

- What did you like and dislike?
- Is anything confusing? Did anything make you pause, even for a second, to understand what I meant?
- Within the context of the story, do the characters act in a believable way?
- Does the setting seem believable? Could you visualize the world I describe?
- Was the plot believable?
- If you read this in a magazine, what would you think?
- Does the story keep you interested the whole way through?

Use this feedback to decide whether your story is ready for submission. Before you contact any newspapers, magazines, or community organizations, have your critique partners review your query letter and your story. **Don't skip this vital step.**

When you receive feedback, resist defending your work right away. It's okay to ask clarification questions if you don't understand the feedback, but don't argue with your critique partners. Remember, they're helping you out.

Month 3:

- **Days 1-10:**
    - Find other writers and/or teachers who can give you helpful feedback. Ask them to read one of your stories and answer the questions above.
    - Research several magazines and/or online journals that publish short stories. Find those that publish stories similar to yours (e.g., fantasy, mystery, etc.). You'll want to review their submission guidelines to make sure you meet their standards. Also, always read a magazine before submitting to it.
    Sample search string: short story magazines
    - Consider submitting a story to a magazine you already read. You'll already understand what articles they're looking for.

- **Days 11-15:**
    - o Consider the feedback you've received. Is it useful? Do you know what to change? How can you make your story better? Revise your work to incorporate the improvements.
- **Days 16-30:**
    - o Contact local newspapers, community newsletters, and libraries to see if there is any possibility of including your story in the next issue. Remember, treat these opportunities seriously. Write a cover letter and use it in your correspondence. In general, don't contact them by phone unless they say otherwise on their website.
- **Every day:**
    - o Write new short stories. One goal might be to write one every two weeks.

One word of caution: in most cases, once your short story is published by one newspaper or magazine, you need to let any future magazines know that it's already been printed once. In general, you're not likely to sell the same story to more than one publication.

More details on selling the rights to your stories, how to handle simultaneous submissions, and many more topics are included in *Writing Advice for Teens: Writing as a Career.*

When you're reading short story magazines, watch for common elements between stories in each magazine. If you want to submit to a particular magazine, you'll need to identify these items. Does every story:

- End with a twist?
- Have an element of romance?
- Start with a description of the setting?

If any of those answers are yes, make sure yours does too. This will increase your chances of matching what the editor desires.

At the same time, look for what you can do differently from the author you're reading. Watch for opportunities to strengthen your own story. Strong writing will often get published, assuming it meets the magazine's requirements.

Months 4-12:

- **Every day:**
    - o Continue to write new stories and solicit feedback from other writers.
- **Days 1-10:**
    - o Write a query letter and tailor it to three different magazines. If you've published other stories in your local newspaper, community newsletter, or library newsletter, mention it. This may help get your new story published.
- **Days 11-15:**
    - o Mail or email your query to those magazines. Plan to wait at least two weeks for a response. If you don't hear anything for more than eight weeks, assume that the answer is no.

Rejection happens often. That's okay. If you get feedback from an editor, use it to help improve your stories. In most cases, you'll just get a polite "no, thanks" form letter, and it's okay to simply move on to the next magazine.

Don't get discouraged if you get a "no" on your first story sent to a magazine.

Remember, it's just a "no" for that specific story. The same editor at the same magazine may say "yes" to your next submission. Keep trying. If you don't believe in your own writing, no one else will either.

> **Did you know?**
>
> *Harry Potter and the Sorcerer's Stone* was rejected by a dozen publishers before being accepted by the Bloomsbury Publishing House in the UK.

Smaller, local magazines are more likely to publish your early stories, or at least give you more specific feedback on why a particular story won't work for them. I recommend submitting to them first.

Keep in mind that every magazine has different policies on how long it will take them to consider a query. Check the submission guidelines for the magazine on their website.

No matter how irritated you might feel by receiving yet another rejection, remain professional. Never send a nasty email or letter to the editor. This will result in the editor removing you from consideration for any future stories.

On the other hand, always send a thank-you note when your story is accepted. It's a way to help build rapport with editors and help them remember your name in a positive way.

Editors keep track of those who are easy and difficult to work with. Be on the "easy to work with" list. Accept rejection with grace.

Exercise: Your first month's schedule

Create your own plan for your first month. What are you going to accomplish? Take one "big" goal (writing a novel, getting published in a magazine, etc.) and break it down into more manageable tasks.

Make sure to incorporate time for reading in your schedule. What books will help you? Refer to the References at the end of this book if you're looking for ideas. Pick one or two books to read over the course of the next month.

Afterward:

Post your schedule on your bedroom door. Every morning, ask yourself if you've accomplished what you set out to do. If not, figure out how to get back on track. It's okay to put off some things until next month, but don't procrastinate on everything.

Track your progress

So now you've created a schedule that works for you (you *did* create a schedule, right?), and you're ready to focus.

Well, almost. One last thing remains: how to track your progress to make sure you keep moving forward. This is where your writing journal comes in.

There are two main methods of tracking regular writing progress: word count quotas and dedicated writing time. Sure there are other methods (such as the "whenever I feel like writing" method), but if you're going to write every day, you need something more concrete.

So which one is better?

In truth, neither one is better than the other. Each one works, but you need to decide what works for you. There are advantages and disadvantages to both.

Word count quotas:

Benefits:

- Easier to plan when your work will finish.
- Psychological boost when you beat your quota.
- Easy to measure whether you're on track.

Disadvantages:

- When you're struggling, it can take a lot of time each day to hit your quota.
- Word counts don't take into account the quality of your writing. Anyone can write 500 words, but making those 500 words fit into a larger manuscript or article can take much more time.

Dedicated writing time:

Benefits:

- Fixed time box, so you limit how much time you are required to work.
- If you struggle to get words down, you can stop guilt free when the time slot is done.
- Allows you room to edit your work, take out scenes, or add in new ones.
- Writing at the same time every day helps you develop writing as a habit.

Disadvantages:

- Harder to plan when a work will finish.
- If you're on a roll, you may not have enough flexibility to continue working beyond your dedicated writing time.

Ultimately, I've decided to go with a blend of dedicated writing time and word count quotas, with a slight twist.

I focus on writing *scenes* instead of purely using word count quotas, and dedicate time from 9pm-11pm to focus only on writing. This allows me to avoid the trap of only paying attention to the number of words I write, while still making progress every day. Using a scene as a measurement helps me avoid checking my word count every few minutes, and focus on writing usable prose.

That said, I still monitor my word count so I make enough progress toward finishing my writing projects.

Since switching over to this blended method, I've found that I can easily hit my quota of 500 words a day, often doubling that number.

Keep in mind that this is what works for me. You may find it easier to stick with either word count quotas or dedicated writing time rather than trying to blend them.

> **Do what works. If it doesn't work, don't do it.**

While working on my debut novel, *The Caldarian Conflict*, I tried something I hadn't before: tracking my total word count each day, and comparing it to where I wanted to be.

In the graph on the next page, the gray line represents an ideal rate of 425 words per day. The black line represents my actual word count as I worked on my novel. As you can see, I didn't meet my original goal. However, I made progress almost every day towards finishing my novel.

On the days I didn't make progress, I was most likely working on other writing projects. I do write every day, but not always on the same project.

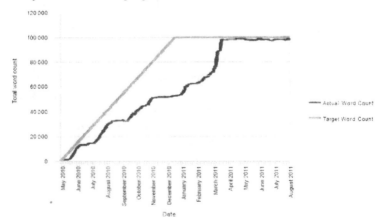

Also, since I updated my spreadsheet every day, I was motivated to add something to the story so I didn't have to record that I made no progress.

You'll also notice that the gray line (my target word count) stopped at 100,000 words. For my novel (in the fantasy genre), 100,000 words is the typical size of a first novel. You can see some fluctuation near the end where my word count hovered around 100,000. Don't make the mistake of assuming the story wasn't changing much. I estimate that I ended up removing around 15,000 words from my original draft, and wrote an additional 15,000 words in extra scenes and sensory detail.

In March 2011, I performed some of the concentration experiments mentioned in earlier sections. You can see how my word counts shot up when I focused on improving my productivity.

Do you have to track your word counts to this level of detail? No. For this story, I found that it helped keep me focused and on task. It might help you too.

You can find a spreadsheet to track your numbers and create graphs at http://writingadviceforteens.com.

What tools should I use?

Write in whatever way makes you feel most comfortable. There are as many ways to write a novel as there are ways to get ready in the morning. Everyone finds his or her own unique approach.

There are lots of tools available that can help writers be more productive. For most short stories or other documents under ten pages, I use OpenOffice Writer (a free Word equivalent). For longer works, I've listed a few of my favorite tools on the next pages, along with why I like them. Check out the websites to learn more about their features.

Please note that I am not affiliated with any of these sites. I'm just a satisfied customer.

Scrivener

Scrivener is by far my favorite tool for organizing writing projects. It has powerful features like a storyboard that let you "zoom in and out" of your novel. For example, you can create virtual notecards that summarize each chapter of your novel and show its current state: to-do, draft, edited, or final (and you can create your own states too).

You can also keep track of various notes and organize them into folders that make sense for you. The interface is also customizable. Want to have two chapters open next to each other so you keep things consistent? Go right ahead!

Perhaps the best feature of Scrivener is that it allows you to create and save templates for future stories. As I worked on this book, I created a general template so I can keep a consistent look and feel across all the books in this series.

Scrivener makes writing easy and fun. I highly recommend it to all writers.

Website: http://www.literatureandlatte.com/scrivener.php

Price: $40 Windows, $45 Macintosh *(prices current as of January 2012)*

LitLift — A Free Novel-Writing Assistant

This website allows you to intuitively organize notes about your books, characters, places, and items. LitLift lets you organize your thoughts so you can focus on the business of writing your book.

Having access to story data from anywhere is a useful feature, especially since you may not be near your primary computer when you have a great idea.

This site is good for those who want to keep notes online and organized in an intuitive fashion.

Website: http://litlift.com

Price: Free *(price current as of January 2012)*

Write or Die!

Besides having an awesome name, *Write or Die!* is also a fun writing tool.

The basic concept behind Write or Die is that you need to make the most of your writing time. In normal mode, the background slowly fades from white to blood red whenever you stop typing. If you stop typing for too long, you get an "annoying sound"–for example, I've heard:

- *Never Gonna Give You Up* by Rick Astley (yes, home of the rickroll)
- Babies crying
- Horns honking

This is a great tool for when you're having trouble getting started with your writing session, have a deadline you're trying to hit, or just to help you fight the temptation to check your email while writing.

Website: http://writeordie.com/#Web+App (iPad and Desktop applications are available)

My settings: 1000 words in 60 minutes

Price: $9.99 iPad App, $10 Desktop Application, Free Web App *(prices current as of January 2012)*

Grindstone

Sometimes, I don't know what I want to write. Instead of writing, I find myself checking my email or surfing the web. An hour or two later, I actually sit down and start writing–then start wondering what's going on with my email again.

Two hours later, I've written ten words and feel frustrated because I haven't gotten anywhere.

Grindstone is a task management application that tracks your work. It also lets you create different profiles so you can organize your tasks into personal, work, or other tasks. I track many of my writing projects using this tool.

Website: http://www.epiforge.com/Grindstone/

Price: Free *(price current as of January 2012)*

STRATEGIES FOR GENERATING IDEAS

*"In writing, there is first a creating stage--
a time you look for ideas, you explore, you cast around
for what you want to say. Like the first phase of building,
this creating stage is full of possibilities."*

—*Ralph Waldo Emerson*

Coming up with story ideas can be a lot of fun. It doesn't have to be stressful. In fact, the best story ideas often come naturally out of what you want to say about life.

In this chapter, you'll find several exercises to generate new story beginnings. Each strategy follows this philosophy: I'll plant the seed, then get out of your way so you can create.

These exercises, or writing prompts, are designed to help unleash the creativity you already have. Some use pictures, and others are just text. The goal is to engage your senses to help you focus your writing abilities. Try them all, and use the ones that work best for you.

Mystery door

The picture on the next page shows an elegant door. However, that's not what makes this photo interesting.

The cool aspect is not even shown: it's what's on the *other* side of the door.

Figure 1: Photo by **tinou**, (**CC license**)

Exercise: The mystery door

Write a short story describing what's on the other side of the door. As you touch the door handle, what do you feel? Does it creak as it opens? On the other side, who do you meet? What interesting objects do you find? Is this a portal to a throne room, or another world?

Afterward:

Consider where your story might go next. Are you set up for a mystery? A romance? Something else?

Jot down any ideas for how the story might progress, and set this story beginning aside. In the next chapter, you'll learn about strategies to turn this beginning into a fully-formed story.

Consider trying this exercise again, but change one detail to start. The possibilities are endless. For example, when you walk through the door, you might find yourself:

- On the edge of a 50-foot drop
- Splattered with ketchup
- In a dungeon
- On a city street
- In a garden
- Facing a dragon

Write whatever comes to mind. This exercise can be repeated again and again. Your imagination can supply countless

Pro tip: If you encounter writer's block while writing a story, have your characters approach a door. Ask yourself what they'll find on the other side. This will often help you come up with a new direction.

story beginnings. Keep your favorites and craft them into longer tales.

Secrets in the attic

Have you ever gone up in the attic of an old house? It can be a creepy place, full of dust, old boxes, and perhaps even a few ghosts.

Imagine that you're up in the attic when you stumble across an old chest. Whatever is inside will send you on an adventure.

Figure 2: Photo by ninahale (CC license)

Exercise: Secrets in the attic

What story comes to mind when you find an old chest in the attic? What secrets are locked inside? Do you find old letters, a forgotten weapon, or a mysterious orb? Does the box suck you inside and transport you to an alternative world, or trap you inside a spell? Who left the box there, and why?

Afterward:

Consider where your story might go next. Are you set up for a ghost story? A story where you travel to a distant past? A tale of long-forgotten love?

Use this example as many times as you like. Old, forbidden boxes beg you to see what's inside. Your readers will be hooked by this simple concept.

Often, writers are encouraged to think "outside the box". In this case, thinking about what's *inside* the box can be much more interesting. In a story, a box can hold anything—including an entire world.

As an example, in *The Lion, The Witch, and the Wardrobe,* four children push through an old wardrobe to find themselves in the magical land of Narnia. This strategy really works!

Pro tip: If you're stuck while writing a story, consider what would happen if your characters discover a mysterious box. What might they find inside? Will it help or hinder them? Who wants to stop them from opening the chest?

Let your imagination run wild, and see what interesting stories emerge from your own box in the attic.

One-sentence prompts

The one-sentence prompt is a classic story generation strategy. I have written two novels and countless short stories initially inspired by a one-sentence prompt, so it definitely works.

Use the one-sentence prompt as a launch point for your story. You can incorporate the sentence into your story if you like, but you don't have to.

```
Example prompt:

A girl prepares for her high school prom.

Response 1:

I was adjusting the strap of my dress when
my phone beeped. A new text message. I
flipped open the phone and smiled when I
read, "Hey QT, C U soon!"
```

```
Response 2:

My phone buzzed on the counter as I was
applying mascara; I hated when it did that.
Luckily, I had just been pulling away, so I
didn't poke myself in the eye like I
usually did.

It was probably Cindy, letting me know she
was on her way to pick me up for the dance-
-there were several of us going together
since none of us had dates.
```

The two examples use the same event: the girl is preparing for her prom when a text message interrupts her. When using a prompt, I usually think about something happening to the character while the event occurs.

Exercise: One-sentence prompt

Choose one of the following writing prompts. Take five minutes and write a short story that uses the prompt as a launching point.

- A warrior fights the battle of his life.
- A teenager prepares to take his driver's license exam.
- A ghost wanders alone through a cemetery.

Afterward:

Feel free to expand the story as much as you wish. When you've finished, set your work aside and edit it in a few weeks. After you've revised your work to the best of your ability, ask your critique partners or writing group for feedback.

Prompt Matrix

This is similar to the one-sentence prompt, but allows you a little more freedom. Construct a "matrix", or grid, of choices, perhaps like this:

Character(s)	Location	Question
Vampire	Science Lab	How did (character) get to (location)?
Robot	Swimming pool	What happens when (character) goes to (location)?
Wizard	Girls' / boys' bathroom	Why does (character) want to leave (location)?
Teenage girl	Castle	Who does (character) least want to see at (location)?
Murderer	Football field	How can (character) escape (location)?
Teenage boy	Walking on a tight rope	Why is (character) at (location)?

With a matrix, you get the opportunity to choose one item from each column to start. If you get stuck, go back to the matrix and pick another item from any column. This is a great way to explore a new world that you've created.

Occasionally, you may have trouble combining two sections. This strategy works really well to help you imagine ways to connect parts of your story together.

Example response:

"I've got to get out!" Joe cried.

His hands slipped on the doorknob. He held his hand up in the dim light.

It was red.

Joe's head dipped in despair. *She deserved better than she got.*

Finally the knob turned, and Joe burst out of the castle into an open field.

Behind him, a horn blew.

In the above example, I first chose Joe (a teenage boy), a castle, and asked why he would want to leave the castle. I borrowed a couple of other concepts (the murderer and the field) as I went, and astute readers might also recognize that I used the door strategy from the first exercise in this chapter.

Likewise, feel free to combine and adapt strategies to help yourself create interesting stories.

Consider using a matrix like this to list the names of several characters and locations from your story. This allows you to create different connections you might miss by just writing your story from beginning to end.

Exercise: Prompt matrix

Use a prompt matrix to start a story. Feel free to use the table above or create your own. Pick one character, item, and question to answer, and then start your story. If you get stuck, go back to the matrix. Have your first character meet a second character, move your character from one place to another, or answer a different question.

Afterward:

Put your story aside. In a week, read your story and mark the places that feel awkward or forced. Rewrite those sections so that they sound smoother or more believable. Once you think your story is perfect, ask your writing partners or critique group for feedback.

History prompts

History is full of fascinating stories: tales of mystery, romance, and adventure. When you're working on your own stories, you can often look to history for inspiration.

While you can base your stories on fact, the cool thing about writing fiction is that you can change any details you like.

Let's take the example of the Lost Colony of Roanoke. Here's a quick version of the basic story. If you're interested in finding out more, feel free to search on the Internet for "Lost Colony of Roanoke".

Roanoke, Virginia was one of the early colonies in the United States, first settled in 1585. By 1587, all of the colonists had disappeared—including 90 men, 17 women, and 11 children. The settlement had been carefully dismantled, and the only clue to where they had gone was a single word carved into a nearby tree: "Croatoan". The colonists were never found, and disappeared from recorded history.

What happened to those colonists? Were they attacked by a tribe called the Croatoan? Did they move to the nearby Croatoan islands? Were they absorbed into nearby tribes?

Nobody knows.

While the story is interesting in its own right, there are dozens of other ways this story could be taken. Here are a few examples:

- *Imagine the future:* Take the basic storyline, but instead the colony is on Mars or some other distant planet. Imagine you're on a supply ship that comes five years later, and the colony has been abandoned. How do you figure out what happened? Do you return to Earth, or attempt to reconstruct the settlement? What messages do you send back to Earth?
- *Imagine today:* During a big storm, you're talking with a friend. Without warning, you're disconnected. The next day, there's no answer. You go over to your friend's house, but it looks like they moved out during the night. How would you find them? What might have happened?
- *Imagine an alternative:* Pretend that you went to visit Roanoke Island today. Perhaps you are visited by ghosts; undead spirits of the lost colonists. Perhaps a wormhole opens and the settlers emerge, tossed through time. Perhaps aliens drop off the settlers after putting them through four-hundred years of experimentation.

Again, the possibilities are endless. When you're writing fiction, you can take stories wherever you want them to go.

Alternatively, you might imagine how life might change if events had taken a different turn. Let's take a big event, such as the nuclear bombing of two Japanese cities, Hiroshima and Nagasaki, at the end of World War II. Consider how history would change if one of the following events had happened instead:

- *The bombs were duds:* Instead of blowing up and killing the estimated 220 thousand lives, the bombs fell harmlessly into the sea. World War II may have continued for another five years or longer. What would the consequences have been? How many more people might have died?

- *While the bombs were en route, President Truman convinced Japan to end the war peacefully:* Admittedly, if you look at the history, this would have been unlikely at the time. However, let's consider what would have happened with a peaceful surrender. Today, Japan is the model of a peaceful nation. Much of this was a consequence of the conditions of surrender they had to sign—Japan can only maintain a military for defensive purposes. How might life be different now if Japan had remained as aggressive? Would Hawaii now be under Japanese control?

- *Just before the bombs drop, aliens contact Earth for the first time:* In this fictional scenario, how would humans react? The entire world is at war—would the attack shift to the aliens? Would we want to work together to seek peace since we're not alone in the universe? How else might priorities change?

These are just a few ways that history might have gone differently. (Okay, some are more likely than others). These ideas give you examples of how to create stories from historical fact. What can we learn from the lessons that history teaches us? Can we spin history in another way to teach others something new?

> **Exercise:** Learn from history
>
> Take one of the examples listed above and create a story around it, or choose another historical event and use similar concepts. Do some additional research on the time period to add historical details to your story, such as names and locations.
>
> For your first draft, don't worry about getting all of your facts right, but ensure that the story makes sense.
>
> **Afterward:**
>
> Put the story aside for at least a week. Come back to it later and see if there are other details that you might want to add, or facts that you want to check. After you've revised your story, share it with your critique partners and get their feedback.

Current events

As I've mentioned before, I read a lot. Since I enjoy writing fantasy and science fiction, I'm always watching for cultural changes and scientific advances that might inspire new stories.

For example, recently I've been watching lots of technical advances in robotics. Some robots are now composed of modular parts similar to LEGO bricks. This means robots can rearrange their own bodies (or even separate and recombine) to overcome obstacles or recover from damage. Several television shows have explored intelligent, modular robots like the Replicators shown in *Stargate SG-1* and the Cylons in *Battlestar Galactica*. By staying aware of updates in scientific advances, you might figure out alternative uses of technology that affect our world in unpredictable ways, or realize potential consequences of the technology (or next steps) before anyone else.

I also recently read a news article that described how over 5,000 blackbirds were suddenly found dead–which reminded me of the events described in *FlashForward* (the TV show, not the book).

Not long after, another article appeared, describing how over 100,000 dead fish were discovered floating in a river only a hundred miles away.

The experts say that these two events are unrelated.

As a writer, I ask, "What if they *are* related?"

Already I have dozens of ideas racing through my head on possible storylines stemming from this:

- Pollution from a chemical plant is killing off wildlife
- Someone poisoned the fish, which then killed off the birds when they came to feed
- A meteor crashes in a nearby lake that releases a deadly amoeba-like creature into the water

I'm sure you get the picture. Dozens of scenarios could have caused these events, or these occurrences could foreshadow other dire problems to come.

While I'm most interested in technology and science, you may be more focused on politics, entertainment, or the economy. My point is that you can use articles from current events to help keep your story relevant.

Writing about a bunch of rebels trying to overthrow their government? Watch for news about uprisings to add an extra layer of realism to your story.

Writing about the life of an artist struggling to become famous? Watch for entertainment stories that describe how others did it.

Writing about the effects of a bad economy on an average family? Watch for stories about people who are laid off from their jobs.

By studying current events, you can improve your understanding of a situation, which helps you write more believable stories.

Exercise: Inspiration from current events

Go to your favorite news site or newspaper. Find an article that interests you, and imagine where the story might go next. Can you change events to make an interesting story? If an expert says that something is impossible, ask yourself "what if it's not?" If someone's life has been devastated by an event, ask yourself "how will they recover?"

Afterward:

Consider what other actions might have caused the events in your article. What happens if the story was influenced by a ghost, vampire, or alien? You might be able to get four or five different story ideas out of the same article.

Still life

You may have heard of artists painting "still life" portraits. In these images of everyday objects, artists work to capture the lighting, texture, and coloring of the subject. In a similar manner, writers often describe objects so the image is clear in the reader's mind.

Find a nearby item that captures your interest. Describe it in as much detail as you can. For example, include the object's:

- Size, shape, color
- Smell, taste, sound
- Value, age, weight

- Texture
- Ability to move
- Flaws, history, uses

Additionally, ask yourself:

- How does it make you feel?
- What memories does it evoke?
- What does this object mean to you or your characters?

Here's an example of what you might end up with.

> This ceramic bookend is unique; I doubt
> there are any others like it in the world.
> It was handmade in 1984 by my mother, who
> lovingly etched my name in the bottom.
> Garfield, that fat, lazy cat, holds up two
> brown books, their pages rough under my
> fingers. Garfield sneers, perhaps
> considering pouncing on Odie as he comes
> around the corner. The ceramic clay is cool
> and smooth as glass. The level of detail
> shows great care—-even the individual teeth
> were shaped by hand.

> Perhaps the one flaw in this bookend is
> its weight. Although heavier than it looks,
> the bookend slides away when something
> heavy leans against it. The bookend is
> hollow and has a small hole in the bottom,
> which means I might be able to fix this
> shortcoming by filling the bookend with
> sand.

> This bookend means even more to me now,
> as its companion was irreparably smashed a
> couple of years ago. It sits safely on a
> shelf, hopefully out of reach of accidental
> damage. As a sign of my mother's love, I'll
> treasure it forever.

Astute readers will notice that I didn't include taste or smell of this object. There's a reason for that: I couldn't smell anything, and couldn't bring myself to taste it. I have my limits, and I'm sure you do too.

This paragraph isn't interesting because of my description of the bookend. The reader is drawn in because of the object's meaning to the author, not the object itself.

Exercise: Still life

Find a nearby object that captures your interest. Describe it in detail, considering the items listed above. Aim for completeness, but if one aspect seems unimportant, feel free to leave it out.

Afterward:

Have a critique partner unfamiliar with the object read your example. Can she visualize it? Ask her if there's anything that seems to be missing.

Show her the object. Does it match her expectations? Are the differences important?

Unusual uses for everyday objects

Some of the most fascinating story ideas come from something ordinary. Is that a mangy old boot or a Portkey? Is that a flower or some mysterious creature? Is that a book or an instantaneous imagination transportation device?

Pick out a mundane object—the best items are those you rarely think about. What else might it be used for? What if you add some magical properties?

Instead of describing it in detail, like in the previous exercise, make the object more interesting by using it in an unusual manner. You might come up with something like this:

```
    Faeries sure are crafty creatures. For
the past century, they've convinced humans
to create an intricate, interconnected
network of copper mesh designed to
transport faeries anywhere in the world.

    What do humans call this network?
Electrical wiring.

    Faeries can access the network through
access points called sockets. In return for
setting up the network, faeries allow
```

humans to use mystical energies to power
certain devices.

Since the energy used is governed by
precise mathematical equations, humans
typically ignore faerie involvement in the
matter. Which is just as well, since most
faeries prefer to avoid advertising their
presence in people's homes.

In this example, I've taken an ordinary object—an
electrical socket—and added magical properties that may
inspire lots of other story ideas.

You don't have to make something magical to be creative.
You can keep your characters firmly rooted in the real world
and show their intelligence by finding a unique solution.

For example, a cup typically holds a liquid of some sort.
However, you might also:

- Tie the cup to a string and swing it like a pendulum
- Smash the cup and use the shards as a primitive knife (in a survival situation)
- Hold it to a wall to hear a conversation on the other side

If you want some inspiration, watch an old TV show called
MacGyver. In each episode, he used everyday materials to
solve real problems. You'll learn a lot.

Exercise: Old dog, new trick!

Look around your room and pick a normal,
everyday object. List five ways you could use the
device differently from its intended use.

Afterward:

Write a short story where your main character
uses the everyday object to get around an
obstacle.

Diseases

Vampires, like all creatures of fiction, are based in reality–real events, real symptoms, and real people. Without access to today's technical resources (like the Internet), people tried to explain these events based on their own experiences–giving birth to the tale of the vampire.

Writers can learn from this. Take advantage of your imagination and come up with a different way to explain the symptoms of a disease.

The legend of vampires came from a mixture of misinterpreted events:

- Vlad the Impaler and his legendary cruelty
- Burying people who were not dead
- Animals that feed on blood and/or transmit rabies

I came up with this theory on my own, but found that dozens (if not hundreds) of doctors and scientists beat me to the punch. Even so, it's still satisfying–those dozens or hundreds of people provide support for my opinion.

While the other doctors and scientists were inspired by a Dracula movie, my inspiration came from an episode of *House* that portrays a woman with rabies symptoms. Among the rabies symptoms shown in the film were:

- Aversion to light and water
- Aggression–biting and drawing blood
- Immunity to pain
- Bats flying away from the infected woman's living space

These symptoms (and others) combine to create a recognizable image of the modern vampire.

Biting/sucking blood

Vampires are perhaps best known for their tendency to bite victims and drink their blood. Occasionally, this will turn those victims into vampires themselves.

Rabies is often transmitted via a bite from an infected creature, like a bat. After a sufficient incubation period, the victim demonstrates rabies symptoms themselves. By the time rabies symptoms are present, the victim is usually not treatable with today's medicine. With only a few rare exceptions, rabies results in death.

Creatures of the night

Vampires are traditionally known to attack during the night. Their victims, often asleep, are at their most vulnerable.

Rabies victims experience photophobia (fear of light), which often causes them to turn away from the source, hissing with bared teeth.

It's easy to imagine a vampire movie at this point, with Dracula (or some other vampire) turning away. I'd also imagine that the idea of using a cross to defend oneself against vampires was accompanied with a bright torch–and this would certainly cause the rabies victim to turn and run.

Garlic and Holy Water

Traditional defenses against vampires include cloves of garlic and holy water. These defenses actually would have worked.

Human rabies victims experience hydrophobia (a fear of water) and a hypersensitivity to strong smells. Garlic and water would have certainly repelled any perceived vampires.

Transforming into Bats

Vampires are often said to have the ability to transform themselves into bats and fly away to escape capture.

Bats are also known carriers of rabies infections. It's easy to imagine coming upon a sleeping victim, only to see a bat flapping away into the night. With other rabies victims (or vampires) already known in the area, it would have been easy for people to assume that a vampire transformed into a bat.

Super-human strength

Vampires are known for being impervious to pain. This gives them the appearance of having superhuman strength, ignoring or shrugging off blows that would seriously injure a normal person.

Rabies victims also become immune to pain as the disease progresses. In the *House* episode mentioned earlier, the victim is hit with a Taser, and feels no pain. For people who had more primitive weapons, it's easy to imagine that rabies victims would appear to have superhuman strength.

Rising from the dead

Vampires, of course, are known for being undead (more active than zombies, but still sustained by human blood).

Some symptoms can be explained by the natural decomposition process, which can make the body appear fuller with blood around the mouth. This may also be partly explained by someone who was accidentally buried alive, which horrifyingly enough, did happen from time to time.

As you can see, even though vampires are fictional, there's a basis in reality. If you're looking to create a new creature, it may help to take symptoms of a disease and use them to guide the creation of a new paranormal race. These traits can help you create believable trends and guide you in creating more realistic characters.

If you happen to write about vampires (as it seems many people are), then you might research rabies to guide your story.

Exercise: Zombie disease

Do some research and find a disease that matches symptoms zombies typically have. For example, zombies typically shuffle, avoid well-lit areas, and eat brains (probably a form of cannibalism). Where do you think the disease came from? Perhaps you'll have to combine a couple of diseases to address all the symptoms (don't forget about decaying flesh). You might also look at fungal infections that alter the minds of its victims.

Afterward:

Find a disease with interesting symptoms, and create a creature that takes them even farther. Is the disease typically transmitted by an insect bite? Perhaps your creature transforms into that insect. Does the disease cause hallucinations? Perhaps your creature can see the future. Your imagination is the limit!

STORY CONSTRUCTION

"Actually ideas are everywhere. It's the paperwork, that is, sitting down and thinking them into a coherent story, trying to find just the right words, that can and usually does get to be labor."

—Fred Saberhagen

For many writers, the difficulty isn't in generating story ideas. The hard part is turning story ideas into well-told tales.

> **Precaution**
>
> I'd recommend keeping copies of your stories everywhere...in hard copy, emailed to yourself, on flash drives, hard drives, etc. The last thing you want is to lose everything and have to start over from scratch.
>
> Backing up your work once a day is best—it's good to make this part of your writing routine. That way, you never lose more than a day's worth of work.

Core concepts

While every story is different, they share many common threads. Understanding how to weave the threads together will help you spin your story into a unique tapestry.

Every story contains:

- Characters – Who the story is about
- Perspective – Who narrates the story
- Setting – Where the story takes place
- Plot – What happens to the characters and setting

Your job is to weave these aspects together to create an interesting tale.

Meet your characters

Picking your characters is one of the most important choices a writer makes.

Done well, characters will find a special place in your reader's hearts. Believable characters are relatable and react realistically. They should seem like someone you might meet on the street.

On the other hand, if your characters feel unrealistic, annoying, or whiny, your readers won't stick around long enough to find out what happens to them by the story's end.

Many authors suggest that you fill out character sheets for every character in your book. These sheets help you keep track of your character's appearance, habits, and feelings. More importantly, these sheets help you better understand your characters, perhaps before you've written a word. For your convenience, an example character sheet is included in *Appendix B.* Feel free to search on the Internet for other examples. There are many other character sheets out there.

> **Did you know?**
>
> *Main characters* are those who the story is most focused on, and the story is usually told from their point of view.
>
> *Major characters* include the antagonist and other important people in the story, but they don't tell the story.
>
> *Minor characters* often show up in just a few scenes and are often in the background. They generally do not affect the storyline, and may not even have a name.

When using character sheets, be careful. The last thing you want to do is to include every detail on your sheet in your story, especially as a laundry list. Keep the details to a minimum—a few good details are a lot better than a lot of unimportant ones.

I've seen poorly introduced characters more times than I'd like to admit. Here's an example I wrote, loosely based on a real book. At what point do you want to skim and find out what happens?

"Stop right there, Alan Markham!"

Alan froze. There was no mistaking that voice. That authoritative voice. His principal, Mr. Durheim, only used that tone when someone was really in trouble.

Mr. Durheim was your typical high school principal. Stern, middle-aged, tall and imposing, always wearing dress shirts that were just a little too tight. He was in pretty good shape, too. Ben, one of the guys on the track team, tried to run away from school last year, but Mr. Durheim had no trouble catching him.

Alan sighed and turned around.

Sure enough, Mr. Durheim's eyebrows were arched in a menacing grimace. His hawkish nose drew a nice firm hook, but even that feature was masked by the anger flashing in his gray eyes. Six-foot-four and easily over two-hundred-fifty pounds, all muscle, even the football players stayed out of his way.

And now he headed for Alan.

Mr. Durheim's loafers tapped against the tiled floor as he bore down on Alan. His tan slacks, neatly pressed, snapped angrily with every step. His dress shirt bulged, threatening to snap the buttons with every irritated breath. His dark blue tie swayed back and forth like a snake waiting to strike.

If you're like most readers, you probably got halfway through that sample and thought: "Come on, already. I know enough about the principal. Why are you taking me through every detail of this guy's appearance?"

Here's what you probably want to know: what did Alan do? Why is Mr. Durheim so angry?

As I've helped dozens of new writers, this mistake happens again and again. The text itself is fine. There are no apparent grammatical errors, and each individual sentence is interesting enough. The mistake is what is called "overwriting," and most writers do that from time to time. The trick is to catch it before it annoys your readers. Your critique group should be able to tell you if you've gone too far.

Here's the same example, cutting down to what the reader really needs to know.

> "Stop right there, Alan Markham!"
>
> Alan froze. There was no mistaking that voice. That authoritative voice. His principal, Mr. Durheim, only used that tone when someone was really in trouble.
>
> Alan sighed and turned around.
>
> Sure enough, Mr. Durheim's eyebrows arched in a menacing grimace. With a hawkish nose and muscled physique, even the football players stayed out of his way.
>
> And now he headed for Alan.

In this case, most of the sentences remained the same. I kept the strongest details and discarded the rest. Readers today have watched tons of movies and have their own experiences with high school principals. They have a lot of images to pull from.

In the second example, my vision of Mr. Durheim won't match yours, but that's okay. The important thing isn't how Mr. Durheim *appears*, but what he *does*.

Detailed character sheets should only be done for your main characters. Major characters should use a shorter version of the character sheet, and minor characters may not have a character sheet at all.

Exercise: Meet your main character

Take a story that you've written and identify the main character. For that main character, answer every question on the character sheet in *Appendix B*.

Afterward:

Read your story again. Do you find any inconsistencies with your main character? Are there any interesting details you could sprinkle into your story? Do you see opportunities to expand your story in new directions to unveil more of your character to the reader?

Also, if character sheets don't work for you, don't use them. It's valuable to try the exercise at least once—that way, you understand the technique and have a new tool to use when you're stuck.

Each character is unique

When writing characters, each one should sound and act a little different. There's nothing more confusing than reading a story where every character sounds the same. Each character should have his or her own dialogue "fingerprint", which is made up of phrasing, word choices, and delivery.

Perhaps your character uses "For sure" to indicate agreement instead of "Okay" or "Yes". Another character might always speak in complete sentences, or another might always feel the need to correct others. Think about the people you know, and the phrases they love to use. You might be able to borrow the phrase and lend it to a character.

Unlike the rest of the narrative, dialogue can ignore some grammar rules. Dialogue should reflect what characters would likely say. For example, consider this dialogue:

"Hello, Nancy. How are you today?"

"I am very well, thank you for asking. How is Bill?"

Pretty boring, eh? Does anyone actually talk like that? Let's try this again.

"Hey, Nancy. What's up?"

"Not much. How's Bill?"

This second attempt is unlikely to win any awards, but at least the pacing is much more realistic.

Into the Land of Iowah. another novel of mine, focuses on the unlikely pairing of a wizard and a truck driver. Consider this set of dialogue. Notice how it's always clear who's speaking, even when there are few dialogue tags. Can you guess which one is the truck driver?

> **What are dialogue tags?**
>
> The most common dialogue tags are "said" and "asked". These words describe how dialogue is spoken, and can include fancier words like "exclaimed", "shouted", or "pontificated". But please don't use "pontificated".

"Ya got a name, buddy?"

"Vagus."

"Vagus," Bob rolled the word. "Strange name."

"Given by my parents."

"Yeah. Ya don't get to choose 'em." Bob nodded sympathetically. "So where ya from?"

"Far from here. A place called Ammanur."

"Ah," Bob said. "Somewhere in the Middle East then, eh?"

"No, not exactly."

As a wizard, Vagus always speaks formally. He remains clear and succinct.

On the other hand, Bob is much more relaxed with his use of language. Bob tries to relate the strange words "Vagus" and "Ammanur" to his experience, relying on what he's seen in the news to guide his thought process.

This, of course, is an extreme example. It's not often that you'll combine two completely different characters like this, but the concept is the same. For example, some people like to make bad jokes, while others might toss in unnecessary words from time to time.

> ```
> "Like, did you see her new highlights?
> She looks like a frickin' skunk!"
> 
> "Totally."
> ```

Who's speaking in the dialogue above? If you guessed a couple of teenage girls, you're right!

Listen to the character's voices. Say the dialogue out loud to check the flow. Does it sound realistic?

Each character also should have different goals in mind. One girl might want to go to a party, while her friend would rather stay home with a book. One guy might like a girl romantically, while she thinks of him as a friend. With different goals in mind, your characters will naturally make different choices that add tension.

Character triangles add tension

Setting up a trio of characters, each with differing goals, can add great tension to your story.

Perhaps the best example I've seen of a good character triangle is in *Bunnicula*, by Deborah Howe. After a bunch of vegetables mysteriously turn white, Harold the dog and Chester the cat are convinced that Bunnicula the rabbit is a vampire, sucking the color from the veggies.

The story has great tension because each character in the triangle has differing goals:

- Bunnicula – Just wants to eat
- Chester – Wants to kill Bunnicula to protect the family from white vegetables
- Harold – Sees no danger from Bunnicula, so he tries to stop Chester from killing Bunnicula

These conflicting goals allow lots of great tension as Chester enlists Harold's help in figuring out whether Bunnicula is a vegetarian vampire. By the end of the story, Harold's loyalty shifts toward protecting Bunnicula, which alters the balance of power.

Character triangles show how different goals cause alliances to change throughout the course of the story. It also shows how each character exploits the flaws of others.

Every character has a weakness

Every character should have some kind of weakness, or flaw. Perhaps the flaw is obvious, such as a character who has problems controlling his anger or habitually cheats on his girlfriend. Characters with these traits are often hard to like.

Flaws don't need to be a negative thing. Perhaps they're too curious, or too focused on adhering to rules. In any case, flaws make characters interesting.

Consider Hermione from the *Harry Potter* series. She's well-known for her intelligence and near-photographic memory—both good things. However, at least in early books, she's too focused on following the rules, and the other students avoid her because of it. Understandably, she's hurt by this revelation, and this nearly gets her killed when a troll breaks into Hogwarts.

Not only should characters have flaws, but other characters should work to exploit those flaws. In *Back to the Future II* and *III,* Marty McFly bristles whenever someone calls him "chicken". This single word is enough to force him into making bad decisions—Marty always wants to prove that he's not a coward, regardless of how stupid the decision might be. The other characters know of this flaw, so they call Marty a chicken to control his actions.

No person is perfect, so no character should be perfect either. Everyone makes mistakes. This adds flavor to your characters and helps your reader feel like they're reading about a real person.

> ## Good characters evolve throughout the story

Events in our own lives affect us. When someone lies, we're less likely to trust them next time. If a friend shares one of our secrets with others, we hesitate before confiding in him again. On the other hand, if someone helps us, we're likely to return the favor.

Characters should react realistically. If a friend cheats off the main character's test, getting both of them in trouble, the main character should cover his answers at the next test. If an alien points a death ray at a loved one in one chapter, the main character should not act like the alien's best buddy in the next.

Believable characters transform over the course of your story. Ideally, by the end of the story, the main character should have learned enough that he could have avoided

> **What is conflict?**
> Conflict describes the tension within a story. It shows the main character's struggle as she makes choices to achieve her goals.

the problem altogether, or at least solve it more quickly. In other words, characters grow through conflict.

In the French folk tale *The Magic Thread*, popularized by William J. Bennett, a young boy laments over the fact he has to go to school. Lo and behold, a witch appears and offers him a magical ball of yarn. After explaining that the ball of yarn represents all the years of his life, she tells the boy that if he gets bored, all he has to do is pull a silver thread, and time will whoosh right by.

The next day at school, the boy gives the thread a tiny pull, and class is soon over. He eventually realizes that he could skip school altogether and fast forward his life to when he had a job and could marry his love. He gives the thread a sharp tug, and sure enough, time flies by. Whenever he ran into difficulty, the boy pulled the thread, until one day he was an old man, and the ball of yarn had shrunk to a small bundle.

At that point, he realizes he's wasted his life, and that another tug might lead him to his death. The witch appears and asks him how he's enjoyed his life. The boy replies that it passed much too quickly, and that he wished to start over. The witch eventually grants him his wish, and the boy relives his life, grateful for every difficulty and savoring every joy.

On another note, this story may seem familiar to some of you: it also formed the basis for *Click*, an Adam Sandler movie.

Stories become more powerful when the main character transforms. Let your characters grow.

Perspective—who's telling the story

There are three basic perspectives: first person, second person, and third person.

In a **first-person narrative,** the narrator is also the protagonist of the story. In other words, the person telling the story is also the main character. The easiest way to pick out this point of view is the use of "I" to describe the main character.

First-person narratives also tend to be more personal, showing you how the main character feels about the situation. This can effectively draw you into the story as you begin to identify with the main character.

Example: First-person narrative

```
    I cautiously creep toward the wooden
building. Clinking glasses and voices float
out the door, and I hesitate one more
```

```
moment before stepping up the short flight
of stairs and entering the restaurant.

    Spying an empty table, I take a seat.
Good thing there's at least one familiar
restaurant in this strange town.

    A waitress walks up and taps her pad.
"What kind of coke do you want?"
```

In a **second-person narrative,** the narrator turns the reader into one of the characters into the story. This perspective is often used in non-fiction, choose-your-own-adventure stories or songs. The easiest way to pick out this point of view is the use of "you" to describe the reader.

Astute readers will notice that most of this book is written in the second-person narrative, where the advice is targeted toward the reader.

Second-person narratives draw in the reader by making them part of the story. As you experience the story with the other characters (or as you apply advice to your own life), you'll begin to identify with the events as if they're really happening to you.

Example: Second-person narrative

```
    Cautiously, you approach the wooden
building. Clinking glasses and voices float
out the door, and you hesitate one final
moment before you step up the short flight
of stairs and enter the restaurant.

    Spying an empty table, you take a seat,
glad to find a familiar restaurant in this
strange town.

    A waitress walks up and taps her pad.
"What kind of coke do you want?"
```

In a **third-person narrative**, the narrator is not a character in the story. The narrator can be omniscient (or all-knowing) or have limited (only having knowledge of a single character's thoughts and emotions). This perspective is the most flexible of the three, which allows the author the most freedom. The easiest way to pick out this point of view is the use of "he", "she", "it", or "they" to describe other characters.

Third-person narratives tend to feel a little more distant from the reader, so the author must work harder to help the reader identify with the characters.

To show internal dialogue here, I use underlines instead of italics, according to standard manuscript format (more of that in *Writing Advice for Teens: Preparing for Publishing*).

Example: Third-person limited narrative

```
    Cautiously, Bill approaches the wooden
building. Clinking glasses and voices float
out the door, and he hesitates. After a
moment, he steps up the short flight of
stairs and enters the restaurant. Spying an
empty table, he gratefully takes a seat.

    Sure am glad to find something familiar
in this strange town, he thought.

    A waitress walks up and taps her pad.
"What kind of coke do you want?"
```

Example: Third-person omniscient narrative

```
    Cautiously, Bill approaches the wooden
building. Clinking glasses and voices float
out the door, and he hesitates. After a
moment, he steps up the short flight of
stairs and enters the restaurant. Spying an
empty table, he gratefully takes a seat.

    Sure am glad to find something familiar
in this strange town, he thought.

    A waitress walks up and taps her pad.

    Great, she thought. Another tourist.

    She forced a smile. "What kind of coke
do you want?"
```

In a short example, like the above, the story might seem more interesting because we know exactly what both Bill and the waitress are feeling. However, in a longer example, knowing everything can exhaust your reader. In my opinion, it's better to stick with third-person limited because this tells the reader who to root for.

The two most common perspectives used in stories are first person and third-person limited. Most writers pick between those two.

Setting—where it all happens

Stories have to happen somewhere. Readers need to understand the rules of the world—whether it's exactly like ours, or if the characters in the story follow different rules. Is magic allowed? What kind of technology do characters have access to? Is it in a historical setting? Do people follow the same laws?

Establishing the setting is also called "world-building". Building a world takes a lot of work, but readers want it to seem effortless. It works best to pick a couple key details that make your world unique.

Consider this excerpt from *The Caldarian Conflict*, one of my fantasy novels.

```
Mendell's sandals scraped against the
wooden bridge as he followed the guards and
the pirate over the moat surrounding the
prison. Glancing into the water, Mendell
wondered if the rumors of the large, man-
eating fish living there were true.
```

In one short paragraph, we've established that it's warm (Mendell is wearing sandals), the timeframe (the wooden bridge over a moat implies that it's a medieval society), and that they're just outside a prison. Notice how I don't need to say that it's warm or that we're talking about a society with limited technology. I trust that the reader can figure it out.

Even if your story is set in our world, you need to do a little legwork. Setting goes beyond the description of a physical location. If you're using a place from history, you may need to spend some time researching the time period in order to give your story authenticity.

For example, if your character lives in Minnesota and asks for a soft drink, she's probably going to say "pop". If your character lives in Texas, she's probably going to ask for a "coke" (yes, that's a little 'c', not to be confused with Coca-Cola).

Part of the reason I bring this up is from personal experience. While visiting Georgia as a teenager, I had the following conversation with a waitress:

> "What kind of coke do you want, hon?"
>
> I paused. "Um, I'd rather not have a Coke."
>
> "We have lemonade or sweet tea if you want that instead."
>
> "Don't you have Sprite?"
>
> "Nah, we have Pepsi products here."
>
> My face twisted in confusion. "I thought you asked me if I wanted a Coke?"
>
> "Yeah, I did. What kind would you like? We have Pepsi, Lemon-lime Slice..."
>
> "Slice is fine."

I left the restaurant with my soft drink in hand, but feeling like I'd just performed a rendition of Abbott and Costello's *Who's on First?* It wasn't until a few days later that I figured out "coke" was slang for what I called "pop" or "soda".

Why do I bring this up? Knowing the slang used in a specific region of the world can help your story feel more authentic.

If you're basing your story in a town or city that actually exists, look up a map or visit the area. Many online map services allow you to see satellite photos and up-to-date store listings that can add a sense of realism to your story.

That said, I prefer not to use brand names in my stories, especially for online businesses. Not so long ago, Yahoo was one of the top search engines, but now Google is the top. Lemon-lime Slice is now called Sierra Mist. A few years ago, MySpace was a major social networking site—and now

Facebook is the current favorite. In another ten years, the brand names at the top of the chain could be something completely different. By the time you read these words, the brand names listed here could be a distant memory.

It's hard to write in a manner that's as specific as possible while remaining relevant. There are a few strategies I use to avoid being too dependent on brand names:

> **Avoid brand names**
>
> Another big reason to avoid brand names is that it can sound like you're working for their marketing team.
>
> If I constantly say I shop at Old Navy, you might start to wonder whether Old Navy paid me to mention them several times. (They didn't).

- Instead of ordering a Sprite or Slice, as shown in my personal example, my characters usually order a "soda". In my opinion, "soda" is the term least likely to be confused with other requests.
- Instead of "I went to Google Maps to look at Rochester, MN," I would say "I searched online for Rochester, MN and brought up the resulting map."
- Instead of "I logged on to Facebook to check out her profile," I'd say "I searched for her profile."

The main exception to this guideline is when the brands actually do matter. In the above example, readers wouldn't have understood my confusion if I *hadn't* used brand names. You might also use brands to help make the time period feel more authentic.

For your setting, you'll want to include things like:

- Terrain
  - Does this take place in the plains, hills, or mountains?
  - Is the soil composed mostly of sand, silt, clay, or rock?
  - Is this a forest, field, desert, or ocean?

- Sky
  - Is there only one sun? One moon?
  - Are the stars a different color?
  - What color is the sky? Are there clouds? Do they look the same as our own?
  - Do meteors often strike? Are there any threats from the sun (solar flares, etc.)?
- Weather
  - Is it hot or cold?
  - Do they have all four seasons?
  - Is there a time when the area gets a lot of rain or snow? What about droughts?
  - Does this area get powerful storms like hurricanes or blizzards?
- Plants
  - Are there mostly trees, grass, or cactus?
  - Are there any flowers?
  - What about vegetables or fruits?
- Animals
  - What type of wildlife lives in the area?
  - Are any of these animals dangerous to humans?
  - Do people keep pets? If so, what type?
- People
  - Are humans the only intelligent life in this world?
  - Can other creatures speak?
  - What clothes do people wear?
  - What traditions do they celebrate? What are their customs?
  - Does anyone have superpowers?
- Technology
  - Do the characters have access to modern technology?
  - Are they more or less advanced than our world?
  - Is magic possible? Is it allowed?

- Society
  - o Are some people richer than others?
  - o What do they use for money (cash, credit cards, bartering, gems)?
  - o Do most people work? Do robots do everything for them?
  - o Are all races, religions, and genders treated the same way?
  - o Who is in charge (president, king/queen, emperor, etc.)?
  - o What types of buildings do people live or work in?

Do you have to answer all of these questions within your story? No, not necessarily. However, sprinkling well-chosen details throughout your story will help your world feel more realistic.

Earlier, in the character section, we learned how to focus on a few important details so your reader can fill in the gaps. In a similar manner, pick a few important details for your setting.

Beware of "info dump"

One of the risks of answering several questions about your setting is that it's easy to write "grocery-lists" of detail. In *Writing Advice for Teens: Editing,* you'll find many tips for avoiding this common problem.

Please note: There are still some readers who enjoy reading specific, detailed descriptions so they can have a firm image of the setting in their mind. Be aware that in today's society, most people prefer to be given just a few details so they can imagine the rest.

Consider this example that describes a setting surrounding a grocery store:

```
The cement block building of the
supermarket looked just like any other.
Security cameras stood prominently on top
of the roof, a reminder to thieves that
someone was watching. The colorful blaze of
its name, FOODTOWN, bore a stark contrast
```

```
against the bland stone. The store's
automatic doors opened as people
approached, closing soon after they entered
or left the store. The parking lot was
filled with cars; many people had just
gotten out of work and wanted to buy
groceries. The store was stocked with
colorful boxes along with fresh fruits and
vegetables.
```

There's nothing obviously wrong with the paragraph above, but at least to me, it seems boring. Why? I've seen all those details a thousand times before, every time that I go to the grocery store.

Instead, let's try this example:

```
I pulled into FOODTOWN's bustling
parking lot. Bread, peanut butter, jam.
That's all I needed. Bread, peanut butter,
jam.
```

You'll notice here that I didn't bother describing the grocery store. The name Foodtown already tells the reader it's likely a grocery store, and that's confirmed by the character's list. The phrase "bustling parking lot" shows that it's a busy time, but we no longer know that it's

> ### Showing vs. Telling
>
> A common problem in stories is "telling" the reader too much. Instead of saying "The store has automatic doors," you might show the reader the doors by saying "The doors slid open as I approached the store."

after work. That detail can come out later, assuming it's important to the story.

If the world is different than our own, you may need to include more detail. Let's say that Foodtown exists on the moon:

```
I activated my rocket boosters to guide
my vehicle into FOODTOWN's already-full
parking lot. Only twelve more hours before
the sun rose on our side of the moon. That
```

```
would be just enough time to gather
supplies for the next fifteen Earth-days.

    One day on the moon lasts almost thirty
days as measured from Earth. That's fifteen
days of darkness, fifteen days of light.
And it gets hot here—over 225 degrees.
That's why we need radiation shields, and
travel is reserved just for emergencies
during the Moon-day. It's better to stock
up, put up the shields, and wait it out.
```

We still don't know why the main character lives on the moon, but at least we better understand the rules of the world. It's the differences from our world that make it interesting.

The final aspect of setting is the tone (also called the mood or atmosphere). You can use this to give clues to your reader right away about what type of book this is.

Your word choices will help convey the tone right away. For example, let's say I want to convey a sense of spookiness.

```
    I stared up at the mansion. Peeling
shutters sagged from the windows; the glass
had long ago broken away. As long as I
could remember, people had told stories
about flickering lights shining out those
remaining holes.

    And I had to go in.

    Alone.
```

You don't need long to set the tone. In the example, the main character is nervous and clearly thinks the house is haunted. Look at the word choices convey the tone:

- "I stared up..." – This gives a sense that the protagonist is hesitating.
- "Shutters sagged...glass had long ago broken away. " – This shows the reader that the mansion is old and rundown.
- "flickering lights" – Most people will immediately think "the house is haunted" with this phrase.

- "And I had to go in." – For some reason, even though it's against his natural inclination, the main character feels compelled to enter this forbidden place.

If you intend to set a more cheerful tone, use words like "bounce", "light" or "grinned". Careful word choices help you set the mood for your story, and help move your plot along.

Exercise: A bright sunny day

Let's say that instead of fearing the mansion as described above, your main character is excited to enter. How would you describe the setting in a way that conveys excitement instead of fear?

Afterward:

Take out a story that you've written. In what ways can you use the setting to set the tone? Are there important missing details you'd like to add? Enhance your setting by incorporating words that help your reader understand how your main character sees the world around him or her.

Basic plot structure

The plot is the sequence of events that occur in a story. In most stories, the plot is the most vital component; the characters and setting don't matter if nothing ever happens. There are five basic aspects to every plot:

1. Introduction
2. Rising action
3. Climax
4. Falling action
5. Ending

A plot arc describes the flow from a story's introduction to its ending.

While each aspect of the plot is important, be careful. Many beginning writers mistakenly believe that means each part receives equal treatment, perhaps something like the graph below.

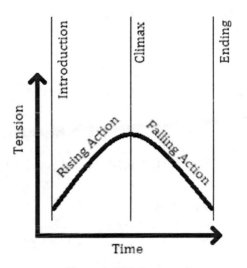

Figure 3: This is wrong!

Stories that follow the curve above tend to be described as too long and boring. Once the story has reached its climax, readers want to finish the book quickly and move on to the next. In reality, most stories follow this skewed trajectory:

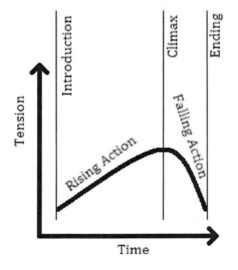

Figure 4: A much more accurate representation

Once your story has made its point, the ending should come quickly after. The falling action should only take a chapter or so, and the ending might take one additional chapter. If you drag things out more than two chapters past the climax, you run the risk of having a story that feels too long.

That said, every story is different. Do what's right for *your* story.

Before you start writing a novel, make sure that you have at least one big, central conflict (and several smaller events or conflicts) to start from. As an example, let's say that I came up with the following story concept for a thriller/suspense novel:

> **Did you know?**
>
> There are two types of literary conflict: internal and external.
>
> *Internal conflict* means that the main character struggles within himself: overcoming addiction, making a hard decision, etc.
>
> *External conflict* means that the main character struggles against outside forces: other characters, nature, society, etc.

```
    Stan Barlow, computer programmer,
discovers his Romanian friend, Liviu
Belieu, dead at work.

    At Liviu's funeral, Stan is approached
by a German scientist who shows him a list
of ten names. Three of the names are
crossed off, including Liviu's.

    Stan's name is next on the list.

    Mistaken for one of the scientists
involved in a secret government program,
Stan flees for his life as assassins
attempt to hunt him down.

    Stan decides he must find and warn the
other targets before they, too, find
themselves at a funeral. Their own.
```

At the heart of plot is conflict. What is your main character trying to do? What prevents him from achieving his goal?

In Stan's case, he will face both internal and external conflicts. Internally, he'll struggle with his grief and need to decide whether he'll focus on saving himself or others. He'll also face threats externally in the form of assassins who want to kill him and others. Stan will show the reader who he is by the choices he makes throughout the story.

Using this example concept, we'll explore how the plot forms. I'll show you my thought process as I work through this design. By the end of this section, I'll have carefully thought through how I'd like the story to go, and easily develop an outline from the results.

Do you need to write a full novel to use this section? Of course not. The basic concepts work just as well for a short story as a novel.

1. Introduction

In the first three to five pages of a novel, today's authors need to do several things:

- Provide a hook (something interesting) to capture the reader's interest.
- Introduce the main character(s).
- Give a strong hint toward the overall plot.

You'll notice this is different from many "classic" novels read in schools. Prior to the 1950s, writers had the luxury of developing complex worlds over the course of several chapters.

The rules have changed.

Today's readers expect action right away. They want to keep engaged throughout the entire story. In some ways, that makes our job as writers tougher, but when you know the rules, it's easier to play the game.

Keep in mind that you can't simply start every story with an explosion. There needs to be a logical connection between the hook and the rest of the story.

Often, you don't need to blow something up in order to hook your reader. Sometimes you can focus on an everyday object. The movies *Nanny McPhee* and *Juno* begin with the camera focused on a chair. *Jack and the Beanstalk* starts with selling a cow for magic beans. *The Fellowship of the Ring* starts with a ring. The objects become a focal point for the story, and it's the meaning behind the object that draws the reader in.

> **What is a hook?**
>
> A "hook" captures a reader's interest. For example, a hook might be a murder, a break-up, or mysterious statue. In literature, a good hook makes a reader care what happens to the main character. Do this well, and your readers will give you time to fill in the holes.

For Stan Barlow (my thriller example), the hook would likely involve Stan's discovery of Liviu's body. How does Stan feel when he sees a friend and coworker slumped over in his chair? Does Stan suspect that Liviu was murdered, or does he assume Liviu had a heart attack? Does Stan call an ambulance right away, or does he try to revive Liviu first?

Starting with a high-intensity event, like a death, allows many opportunities to show aspects of the main character that might otherwise remain hidden. As readers, we get to learn how the main character reacts to pressure. As writers, we have the opportunity to showcase our main character's heroism in a tense moment.

That said, avoid the following cliché, or overused, hooks. They've used so often that today's readers have little patience for them.

Examples of clichéd hooks:

- *The Dream Sequence*—Starting with a dream shows the reader that the main character was never really in danger. This is disappointing, and many readers simply close the book at that point and find something else to read.
- *The Prophecy*—Long ago, the elders foretold that a hero would come to save the world. It's okay to have a prophecy at some point in your story (though I personally avoid them), but don't start with it. Let's get right to the main character and see what's happening in the real story.
- *Here's a Treasure Map*—Having someone (a king, a hunchbacked man in a bar, etc.) send the main character on a quest for treasure or to save a maiden is used far too often. A more compelling example would be for the main character to discover a reason where she needs to go on the quest. Don't have another character tell her what she needs to do—have her decide for herself!
- *The Phone Call*—Someone calls with an important message, and the main character must leave immediately. Instead, skip to the action that shows why the main character must drive the story.
- *Waking up on a Typical Morning*—Showing the same old boring routine, where the main character gets up, brushes their teeth, and gets ready for school or work. Readers are interested in what's different about this character's life, not what's the same.

In a thriller, beginning with a death or other catastrophe sets the tone for the rest of the book. It creates a sense of danger and urgency. Even in the first few pages, you can hint at the overall conflict without giving too much away.

For other genres, use a hook that makes sense. A romance might begin with a nasty breakup, a passionate kiss, or a bucket of half-eaten ice cream. A ghost story might begin with an untimely death, a warning of a curse, or a creepy old house. Figure out what makes sense in

> **What are protagonists and antagonists?**
>
> The *protagonist* is the main hero of the story.
>
> The *antagonist* is the main opponent in the story. An antagonist can be human, a machine, a natural process, or a supernatural being.

your genre by reading lots of examples. Pay attention to how other authors begin their stories. It may give you some ideas about how to start your own.

> **Questions to answer – Introduction:**
>
> - Who is the main character (protagonist)?
>
> - Who or what is the enemy (antagonist)?
>
> - What is the major conflict?
>
> - Where and when does this story take place?

2. Rising Action

Now that you've hooked your reader, the next step is to start your main character down the path to the eventual climax. You'll want to include several events (three to five major events are ideal) along the way. Each event should "raise the stakes" for your main character. Eventually, the story will reach a breaking point.

For Stan, the next major event will be when the German scientist shows him the list that contains Stan's name. With three names crossed off Stan and the reader will assume that he's likely a target too.

How will Stan react to this revelation? Will he panic and call the police? If so, how do the police react? Do they laugh it off? Does the German scientist stop him?

> **Raising the stakes**:
>
> At every step along the way, the main character will become inextricably tied to the plot. Raising the stakes means that the main character feels more urgency to find the answer to whatever questions the story presents.

Other events on Stan's way to the climax might be.

- Finding another person on the list, only to find that the target already died.
- Evading assassins as they attempt to kill Stan.
- Finding another person on the list in time to warn him or her, but unfortunately the target dies anyway.
- Joining forces with another survivor.
- Discovering that the assassins took a friend or family member hostage.

Each event needs to make the challenge more personal for Stan. This will drive him to keep uncovering the mystery.

Eventually, when Stan reaches a breaking point, it's time to bring the story to its climax.

For other genres, you'll need to consider what events make sense within the context of your story. Here's an example of ways to raise the stakes within a romance. Let's assume that the story started with a girl named Sarah observing a cute new boy in class. Events along the way might include:

- The head cheerleader flirts with the new boy.
- The teacher assigns a group project and pairs Sarah and the new boy together.
- Sarah's mom objects to the two meeting at a café, insisting it would look like a date. Instead, Mom

suggests they work on the project at Sarah's house, where they're bugged by a nosy younger sister.

- At the end of the project, the new boy asks Sarah to the homecoming dance.

When you read other stories, take note when the author raises the stakes for the main character. You might get ideas to improve your own tales.

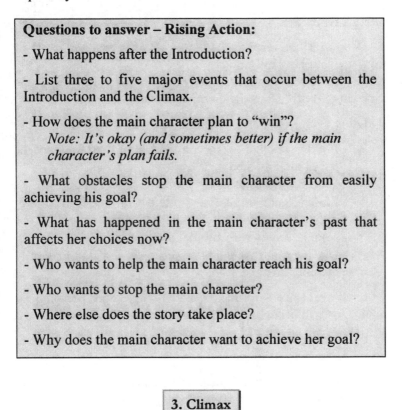

Questions to answer – Rising Action:

- What happens after the Introduction?

- List three to five major events that occur between the Introduction and the Climax.

- How does the main character plan to "win"?
   Note: It's okay (and sometimes better) if the main character's plan fails.

- What obstacles stop the main character from easily achieving his goal?

- What has happened in the main character's past that affects her choices now?

- Who wants to help the main character reach his goal?

- Who wants to stop the main character?

- Where else does the story take place?

- Why does the main character want to achieve her goal?

3. Climax

All the events in your story should lead to the climax. This is where your reader should be on the edge of his seat, waiting for the conclusion.

This is where you'd include the final battle, the point where you catch the bad guy, or that breathtaking first kiss. This is the payoff for your reader—after spending hours or days reading your book, they finally know "what happens."

You might also choose to let the main character realize that she never *really* wanted what she's been chasing. The main character might realize that she is no longer attracted to the new guy, and instead wants a good guy friend to become her boyfriend. She might realize that she wants to go to a different college, or choose a different major. She might decide that her rival is actually the better choice and let the rival win.

> **How long should a climax be?**
>
> The length of a climax will vary for any given story, but usually the climax is contained within a single chapter

These climaxes are transformative: the main character should have grown throughout the course of the story. If the main character doesn't grow, your readers will usually be disappointed by the ending.

For Stan, the story description hints, the climax will be when he evades his own death and uncovers the identity of the assassins. At this point, Stan will discover why the assassins are killing off the others on the list, and understand what to do next. Through the events in the book, Stan will have grown from an everyday computer programmer into a hero.

Look at popular stories for their climax. In *Cinderella*, the climax is when Prince Charming slips the glass slipper onto Cinderella's foot, and it fits perfectly. In *Harry Potter and the Deathly Hallows,* it's Harry and Voldemort's final battle. Watch how other authors handle climaxes, and you'll find strategies to improve your own stories.

Questions to answer – Climax:

- What is the breaking point of the story?
  Note: This usually involves the main character making a big decision between two possible outcomes.
- Who "wins"?

4. Falling Action

After the story's climax, you need to wind down the story. This is where you wrap up loose ends and let the main character process the climax.

Your main character might have won the final battle, but he probably lost something of value. This would be an appropriate place for him to mourn the death of a friend or reflect on something he sacrificed.

While it's rare, your main character may have lost the final battle, or broken up with the cute guy/girl, or failed to solve the mystery in time. Your main character may also have received a fatal wound. Give them time to process the climax—your reader needs the time too.

In Stan's case, he would likely spend time mourning the loss of friends, visiting wounded in the hospital, or perhaps dealing with guilt for not saving everyone on the list. However, he should also feel satisfied that he saved the day by unveiling the assassins and preventing further death and destruction.

When you're reading a book, pay attention to what happens after the climax. You'll often find the real motivations behind character actions here, as well as the resolution of any subplots.

> **What's a subplot?**
>
> With longer stories, like novels, there are often several plots running concurrently. In a romance, you might have a rivalry between two women for the same guy, or a woman might need to choose between her career and love.

You don't have to answer every question in your story, but you should answer most of the big ones. If someone died, let the main character mourn them. If someone acted suspiciously throughout the story, but is actually one of the good guys, the reader should understand why.

The falling action should lead naturally to the ending. At this point, as writers, we want to wrap up the story in a neat little package to give the reader a sense of closure.

Questions to answer – Falling Action:

- How has the main character changed as a result of the climax?

- What happened to the other major characters in the story?

- How does the main character feel about the climax?

- How have relationships changed throughout the story?

- What are the consequences of decisions made in the climax?

---

5. Ending

Endings should satisfy the reader, but ideally should not be predictable. I like to end each of my stories with a final twist that keeps the reader thinking about the story long after they turn the last page. At the same time, the story must remain believable so readers aren't disappointed by a lackluster ending.

Often, endings reflect the beginning. Don't think of this reflection like a mirror. It's more like the rippling surface of a pond. Like the introduction, the ending is usually just a few pages long.

For example, a guy who lives alone at the beginning of the story may have found a girlfriend by the end. A story that

---

What's a twist?

A twist is a way of tricking the reader into believing one thing, but unveiling that something else had really occurred. It might include showing that another, even worse bad guy was actually in charge. It's a fun way to get your readers interested in an upcoming sequel.

begins with a fight might end in a war. One that starts with a physically weak main character might end with him finding newfound strength.

The end of Stan's story could go several ways. He could die from wounds sustained in battle. He could go on to work with the government on other secret programs, or receive a large reward from the government for his contributions in unveiling the assassins.

Before you work on the ending of a story, pick a few of your favorite books off the shelf and reread the last few pages. How did those authors end the book? If the book was part of a series, there's usually a hint of the next story to come. Study how other authors handle their endings, and you'll have a better understanding of how to end your own stories.

Questions to answer – Ending

- Is the main character better or worse off than the beginning?

- What happened to the antagonist?

- What will happen next?
    Note: This could lead into a sequel, or you could imply that the characters live happily ever after.

Exercise: The plot thickens

In the previous section, *Strategies for generating ideas,* you may have come up with a story beginning that you haven't finished. Pull out a story idea and answer the questions listed for the Introduction, Rising Action, Climax, Falling Action, and Ending.

Afterward:

By the end of this exercise, you will have essentially developed an outline for your story. Now your task is to start filling in the details and actually write the story. You're on your way!

Develop a plan (outline)

Now that you understand the basic components of a story, you're ready to develop a plan for your book. If you performed the exercise in the previous section, you already have a great skeleton to start fleshing out for your story.

Why outline?

Outlines help you keep track of a high-level view of your story. As much as authors would like to pretend otherwise, no one can keep an entire book in mind, especially as it's being written.

By completing an outline, you're using a strategy that breaks a long story into manageable chunks. This allows you to more easily understand how a scene fits into the overall story. By asking whether a scene makes sense within the context of your entire story, you don't waste time writing scenes you'll throw away later.

This also allows you to skip around, writing the scenes you find most interesting first. You also have a better idea of where you're at within the story and how much further you have to go.

Don't some authors just wing it?

Yes, some do. Stephen King is a big proponent of the discovery method. Keep in mind that he's also an experienced writer, and has developed an instinctive feel for what makes a story interesting.

Most writers that attempt discovery writing will spend a lot more time editing after completing a first draft. By doing a little bit of planning up front, you'll save yourself countless hours in the editing process.

I'm personally a fan of a "just-enough" outline. A "just-enough" outline tells me the story concept, where the story will start, where it will end, and a few events along the way. For example, as a reminder, here's the basic concept for my story about Stan Barlow

> Stan Barlow, computer programmer, discovers his Romanian friend, Liviu Belieu, dead at work.
>
> At Liviu's funeral, Stan is approached by a German scientist who shows him a list of ten names. Three of the names are crossed off, including Liviu's.
>
> Stan's name is next on the list.
>
> Mistaken for one of the scientists involved in a secret government program, Stan flees for his life as assassins attempt to hunt him down.
>
> Stan decides he must find and warn the other targets before they, too, find themselves at a funeral. Their own.

As I worked through the plot development section, here's what I came up with for an outline:

1. Introduction

   Hook: Stan discovers Liviu's body.

   Questions to answer:

   - How does Stan feel as he sees a friend and coworker slumped over in his chair?

   - Does Stan suspect that Liviu was murdered, or does Stan assume Liviu had a heart attack?

   - Does Stan call an ambulance right away, or does he try to revive Liviu first?

   Additional detail to cover:

   - German scientist shows Stan the list that includes both his and Liviu's name and explains the situation. Stan realizes he is also a target.

2. Rising Action

> Major events:
>
> - Stan and the German scientist join forces.
>
> - Stan and the German scientist track down another person on the list, only to find that the target already died.
>
> - Stan must evade assassins as they attempt to kill him.
>
> - Stan and the German scientist find another person on the list in time to warn him or her, but unfortunately the target dies anyway.
>
> - The assassins kidnap Stan's family and keep them in exchange for both Stan and the German scientist.

3. Climax

> - Stan rescues his family from the assassins, but the German scientist loses his life. I'd like Stan to figure out a way to capture the assassins in the process.
>
> - Why are the assassins trying to kill off the scientists? Are they working for another government? What is their motivation?

4. Falling Action

> - Stan deals with guilt as he mourns those who were lost.

5. Ending

> - Stan returns to Liviu's grave to tell him that the assassins will receive justice.

As you can see, this outline is pretty short. It covers several (but not all) of the questions posed in earlier sections, and only took me about ten minutes to complete.

You'll also notice that I don't pretend to know everything about the story. Instead, I ask myself questions about things I haven't yet figured out so that I can think about them later.

Do I have to follow my outline?

No, of course not! Don't feel like your outline is set in stone. If you decide you want your story to go a different direction, update your outline and keep going.

An outline is just a plan. Plans can change. If you decide the plot isn't clever enough, or feel there's a better way to end the story, you can change the outline at any time. By creating an outline, you have a decent shot of moving the story forward with every scene.

What if I don't know the ending yet?

It's okay if you don't have a perfect ending in mind. Even so, it's still a good idea to have a general idea of where your story is going.

The introduction to *The Caldarian Conflict* came easily for me--a thousand words of action that gave the reader a sense of the intended story. Colors and scents of this new world flashed in my mind like a memory. These first thousand words were easy to write, in a large part because I just had to write down what was already clear in my mind's eye.

Even so, while the intro was compelling and exciting, I struggled with where to go next.

So I compromised.

Instead of planning everything, I planned out the next three chapters. Once I finished those, I took another look at my story, and realized I did have an ending in mind, but I had to write a little to find it.

Once I figured out the ending, I finished my outline. Understanding the basic story structure made a huge difference in my personal productivity.

<u>Why is the ending important?</u>

Once you know where the ending is, you can start to figure out how close you are to finishing your novel. It's something that helps for planning purposes—if you want to finish your book in six months, you should have an idea of what you've already completed and how much farther you have to go.

And now it's your turn.

Exercise: Map out your plan

Using the questions in the section on plot development and the example in this section, create a basic outline for your story. Aim to finish this in less than an hour.

Afterward:

Write your story!

BUILD YOUR STORY,
ONE WORD AT A TIME

TYPICAL WRITING PROBLEMS

"If I waited for perfection, I would never write a word."

—Margaret Atwood

All beginning writers (and most published authors) experience the same problems. With these tips, you'll be able to quickly maneuver around or even avoid them.

Writer's block

Those two words are enough to terrify any writer.

But don't worry.

Writer's block is natural. Every writer experiences it from time to time. And you can learn strategies to work around the dreaded writer's block.

First, relax. You can't be creative when you're stressed.

When you experience writer's block, you are probably having trouble knowing exactly what you want to say. Don't worry about that.

> **What is writer's block?**
>
> Writer's block is a treatable condition that describes the frustration writers experience when they don't know what to write. It often results in blank pages and confusion about where a story should go next.

Instead, think about what's interesting within your story. How would you describe it to a friend? Write down what you'd say.

You don't have to get it right the first time. The purpose of a first draft is to get the ideas down. You can always edit it later.

The *Strategies for Generating Ideas* section will give you several ideas for filling up a blank page or linking two scenes together.

If that doesn't work, try some of the following treatments for writers block.

Treatment #1: Relaxation
(Duration: 3-5 minutes)

Anyone who has been on an airplane has seen the typical safety routine. Passengers are instructed that if the oxygen masks drop, each passenger should secure one's own mask before assisting a child (or anyone else). In a similar manner, writers need to take care of themselves before taking care of their work.

For most writers, in order to create their best work, relaxation is key. I usually close my eyes and imagine a quiet stroll through a forest or walking along a beach. Any imagery will do, as long as it relaxes you. The goal is to (temporarily) stop thinking about the work at hand. In fact, your true goal is to keep from doing anything at all, so that you can approach your work with a clear mind.

After 3-5 minutes of relaxation (or whenever your mind feels more clear), try again. Often, this is enough for me to get moving again. If not, I try treatment #2.

Treatment #2: Try something new
(Duration: 30-45 minutes)

You've tried relaxing, but it didn't work fast enough. What's treatment #2? Essentially, the idea here is similar to treatment #1–you want to get your mind off the current problem (again, temporarily).

Take a short walk, eat a meal with your family, or read a favorite book. Listen to music that fits the "tone" (pun intended) of your story.

If you finish your activity and find that you're still stuck, move on to treatment #3.

> ### Treatment #3: A hint of humor
> ### (Duration: 5-10 minutes)

Spend 5 minutes reading jokes online, or, if you have one, rifle through your joke file. I have several jokes conveniently located above my desk that are guaranteed to make me laugh. You know what makes you laugh...spend 5 minutes reading or watching something funny!

Why humor? Humor breaks you out of your typical operating mode and frees up your creativity. Writer's block often includes the feeling that you lack creativity, so allowing yourself to laugh breaks you out of that box.

> ### Treatment #4: Get started now!
> ### (Duration: will vary)

Enough procrastinating!

Treatments #1 and #2 are procrastination techniques that force you to take a break from working on something you're stuck on. Treatment #3 helps you to think differently. The goal with this treatment is to get something (anything!) down on paper.

At first, just focus on the ideas that you want to get across. Don't worry (right now) about getting full sentences, unless they happen to come to you.

Once you have your ideas down, focus on how you want to put them together. Here's an example.

What I want to say:

> Fish taste good.

Wait…what type of fish? Am I saying all fish taste good? Is there anything else missing that I want to say or imply?

What I want to say:

> Salmon tastes good, and I also like the way it looks.

Okay, this is better, but what do I like about the way it looks?

What I want to say:

> Salmon tastes good, and I love its pink color.

Okay, this seems like enough about the ideas I want to convey. Now how do I want to say it? Let's pick a story form:

> The salmon was delicious--the grilled peach flesh melted in my mouth.

Or let's pick a cooking video:

> Grilled salmon tastes best when it has turned from a dark pink to a rosy, almost peach color, with nice dark streaks from the grill.

Or perhaps even from the perspective of the salmon's spirit:

> My peach flesh was so tender, marked with beautiful streaks from the grill's flames that even I had to admit that, were I still alive, I'd have to eat myself.

Allowing yourself to have fun with what you're writing is the best defense against writer's block.

Also, notice where I started from: "Fish taste good". While that phrase wouldn't have won me any awards, my later attempts grew much closer to something you might actually see in a book.

If this doesn't work, write a poem, email, or a joke. Get something (anything!) down on the page.

The basic concept here is to get down your ideas in some draft form. It might not be pretty at first, but that's okay. Think about two or three objectives you want to accomplish in a particular scene. When you understand your goal and what you want to say, you'll quickly get around writer's block.

The perfect time to write

Many writers find themselves caught in the trap of waiting for the perfect time to write.

Don't wait.

Write now.

The problem with waiting is that, once you start procrastinating, it's hard to stop. Minutes turn into hours, hours to days, and before you know it, years have passed since the last time you sat down to write something new.

Writing is a lot like exercising.

- Once you stop writing, it's hard to start again.

- The more you write, the easier it is.

- Writing every day will make you a stronger writer.

- You might not see results right away, but keep at it. After a month, look back at what you wrote. You'll see a noticeable difference.

Even if you feel like you have no time, try writing something for 15 minutes every day. Take a few moments just before going to sleep, or right after you wake up, to create something new.

Most of all, remember to have fun. Don't worry about getting a full story done, just focus on one scene at a time.

Lately, the main way I've been fitting writing in is at lunch. While eating, I'll spend about 45 minutes dedicated to writing.

If you set a small achievable goal and write at the same time every day, you'll soon settle into a routine that helps you finish your projects.

I had a great idea, but…

Life happens. Hard drives crash, that piece of paper gets lost, or someone interrupts you before you can write an idea down.

There are a few strategies I use when I am afraid I'm going to lose an idea.

1. Whip out my voice recorder

Yes, talking into a machine might make me look like a geek. On the other hand, it's really not much worse than talking into a cell phone. Even better, many phones also have voice recording programs, so you can pretend you're having a conversation with a friend.

That said, my $30 investment has saved me hundreds of ideas, phone numbers, and shopping trips. Any time I think there's the slightest possibility I might forget something, I put it on my voice recorder. When the task is done (or at least copied somewhere else I will check later, like my email), I delete the message.

A voice recorder also works well to record interviews with people who have interesting stories to tell. Before my 93-year-old great-uncle died, I recorded several hours of stories he liked to tell. Though I miss him dearly, it's neat to have a small piece of him still around.

Always ask permission before starting a recording device when talking to someone else—for one thing, it's just good manners. For another, it helps protect you legally, since many states now require that both parties be aware when a conversation is recorded.

The other nice benefit: you get to focus on the conversation, not on taking notes.

2. Mentally attach the idea to something I'm wearing

This is an adaptation of the old "tie a string on your finger" method of remembering things.

For example, I might mentally attach my belt to the idea of an old man, sitting on the top of his stage coach, whipping a horse as he tries to evade bandits closing in from behind.

When I go to take off my belt later that day, I'll be suddenly reminded of the crack of the whip (a belt snapping and a whip cracking sound quite a bit alike). Once I have a good starting point, I'll be better able to remember the rest of the story.

3. Tell someone I'm with enough of the idea that I can remember the rest

If I'm with someone I trust, I might give them a word or phrase that can be used as a trigger to remember the rest of the memory. With two people, it's more likely that at least one of you will remember the phrase.

This can be a bit risky, since I may not always know someone well enough that I can share my ideas. On the other hand, if the other person is a fellow writer, I might even be able to develop the idea in conversation right there.

4. Leave yourself a message

Often, you can excuse yourself from whatever situation you're in and "make a quick call." Instead of calling someone else, call your own voice mail and leave yourself a message.

This way, when you get home, you can check your voice mail and copy down the message at your leisure. Keep in mind that a voice mail is typically limited to sixty seconds or less. It's a great way to cheaply keep from forgetting your ideas.

Alternatively, you might also text yourself, or if you have a smartphone, use an application to quickly jot down your ideas. Since most people have a cell phone, this is a convenient way to save your ideas.

5. Carry a small pad of paper and a pen

Even though I have my voice recorder, I still carry around a pad of sticky notes. Sticky notes are convenient, and it's easy to quickly fill one up with ideas.

A pen and a pad of paper is also useful because you can appear to be taking notes while you're saving an idea to be mulled over at a later time. This allows you to jot down your basic idea and then get back to what you should be doing, such as paying attention to class. I've found I can better focus on classes or meetings when I'm not worried about how to save an idea.

This is also convenient if silence is required. In the middle of class, a religious service, or other meeting, it's often better to take a note than speak into a device.

Help! My computer crashed!

At some point, pretty much every writer loses their work due to a computer failure. Once it happens, there's not much you can do. However, you can limit the scope of the damage by backing up often.

As I mentioned in an earlier chapter, it's a good idea to email yourself a copy of your current project on a daily basis. Alternatively, consider backing up to a flash drive or external hard drive so you can move to a new computer quickly.

Occasionally print off a copy of your manuscript so you have at least one version of the document. This is best done as you approach the end of a first draft so you have as much material as possible, and it also offers you the opportunity to edit your draft. Worst case, you'll have to retype it all by hand.

After a computer crash a couple years ago, I wrote the following story. I hope you find it informative!

My computer crashed last week.

What a frustrating experience! I back up every week, but unfortunately, it crashed on the morning of back up day. A week's worth of work, gone in an instant.

I'm not one to cry, but losing a week's worth of writing is just about the worst experience in the world. I've lost more than that in prior crashes, but I felt worse about this one; I'd thought I was prepared!

Luckily, I'm also pretty handy with computers, so I was able to recover most of my data. It took four hours, but I recovered almost all of the work I'd done over the past seven days.

What a relief!

I've started a new policy: a daily backup. I don't ever want to lose more than a day's worth of work.

In fact, I just kicked it off, so data is copying in the background. I'm feeling much better about--

Before I could finish that thought, the walls begin shaking, and I hear a loud rumble outside. I start toward the window, when the window suddenly starts moving towards me!

I scramble back, under a table, vaguely remembering that was the safest place in case of an earthquake. It seems like a better idea than standing in the middle of the room.

The rumbling finally stops, and the crunching of the broken wood fades into

silence. I slowly crawl out from beneath
the table.

As the dust settles, I make out the
shape of a large dump truck. A small yellow
sign fades into view through the dust:

"Watch for vehicle when backing up."

Crap, I have nothing to do!

Someone cancelled on you, there's nothing urgent on your plate, or you're simply bored. Maybe school is cancelled and you have a snow day. What next?

For the most part, I take advantage of the opportunity and write.

Here are several tasks you can consider when you feel like you have nothing to do. Each of these will help you use time more efficiently and improve yourself as a writer.

Writing task #1: Finish smaller tasks

If you're anything like me, you have several small tasks that you've been putting off for days (okay, weeks or months). Perhaps it's going through feedback from your last critique group meeting, or editing that story you wrote a couple months ago.

Take advantage of the extra time to finish some of the smaller tasks that have been piling up, but were low on your priority list. Cleaning up several loose ends helps you feel like you're effectively using your extra time.

This is also a good thing to try when you encounter writer's block. If you're feeling less creative, sometimes finishing a small task is just the motivation you need to get started with "real" writing.

Writing task #2: Copy notebook entries to your computer

I use a notebook that I update daily with new story ideas, short stories, and dreams from the night before. Instead of checking your email, playing video games, or chatting with friends, take time to catch up on some of your old notes.

Storing ideas in a notebook, while tangible and satisfying, is also difficult to search through. I find it easier to copy the ideas to my computer because it allows me to search for them later.

Writing task #3: Brainstorm ways to incorporate ideas in new stories

After getting back in the mindset of a story idea, I often find there are ways I can expand what I've written into a much larger story, or discover ways to take the idea in a different direction.

For example, I might find a character that, while only showing up momentarily in a story idea, captures my attention. I start thinking about the character's background and the events that might have led up to that moment in the story. Often, these events take interesting twists that are well worth exploring.

While thinking about this, I'll often pull out my outline to play with these ideas. An hour later, I often find myself deep in the creative process, writing or rewriting some aspect of my story.

Writing task #4: Reorganize/prioritize remaining ideas

Make a list of all your story ideas, and mark the ones that seem the most promising. Create a prioritized list for how you plan to finish each story. Estimate the time you need to finish your ideas, and create a schedule to get it done.

If you're just getting started with writing stories, take some time to brainstorm new ideas (perhaps using strategies from this book). If you can't be online, at least you can get some good writing done.

For what it's worth, at this moment I have a prioritized list of twenty book ideas (including this one). Each project is in a different stage—some are half-written, others exist as pages of notes, and others are simply a couple of sentences long. My goal is to complete this list within the next few years.

Is this goal even possible? Maybe, if everything goes according to schedule. Even if I fail to complete all of them, finishing even five books in a few years is a great accomplishment. It's okay to have big goals. You never know what you can do until you try.

Writing task #5: Focus on your best idea

Out of the ideas you've now prioritized, pick your best one and start writing. By solving the minor tasks first, you've already built up a sense of accomplishment, and eliminated some of the tension caused by having those smaller tasks in the back of your mind. In other words, you're in an ideal state to create some of your best work. Take advantage of your momentum and keep writing.

Writing task #6: Read a book

Tons of great writing books are available at your library, a bookstore, or online. Check out the References section at the end of this book for more great books to help you improve as a writer.

My teacher says I'm breaking the rules

First of all, it's important to note that there are certain rules for school assignments, and different rules for writing fiction. To get an "A", you have to follow your teacher's guidelines. If your teacher says that you need to write five to eight sentence paragraphs and at least five words per sentence, that's what you have to do.

While this technique works, it's wrong for fiction, or at least, it's not always right. The real trick to writing a good paragraph isn't whether you follow a template. It's whether you can write paragraphs that are captivating, cohesive, and coherent.

Most English teachers recognize that there are different rules for stories and for school work. Even so, there always seem to be a few who forget to remind students about this detail.

Here are the rules you should follow for writing fiction:

> **1. Each paragraph should focus on one topic**

Finding good places to separate your paragraphs can be difficult. However, there are some things you can do.

One trick I use is to identify when I need a new paragraph is to determine when I'm talking about more than one topic. If there's more than one topic, I split a paragraph apart. Generally, this means my paragraphs are between two and four sentences long, not five and eight.

In dialogue, keep to one character's actions per paragraph. For example, instead of:

```
"Can I use more than one character in a
paragraph?" I asked. Sarah frowned. "No, it
gets confusing."
```

Try this instead:

```
"Can I use more than one character in a
paragraph?"
```

```
Sarah frowned. "No, it gets confusing."
```

In this case, two paragraphs make the story a lot more clear. We know who's speaking, and we know exactly what's going on. One keystroke makes all the difference.

2. Shorter is better

People don't like to read long paragraphs. Big blocks of text can be intimidating.

Instead, keep your paragraphs short, especially for long stories or content written for the Internet. Making your work easy to read is the first step to getting your message across quickly.

Use short paragraphs to emphasize an idea, create tension, or make your reader pause.

Which of the two examples below is more exciting?

```
    I dashed around the corner and leaned
against the wall, catching my breath.
Footsteps sounded around the corner.

    Crap. He's still coming. Where to next?
Glancing up, I saw an open window. The
footsteps came nearer. No choice, I
thought. Up I go.
```

Or this:

```
    I dashed around the corner and leaned
against the wall, catching my breath.

    Footsteps sounded around the corner.

    Crap. He's still coming.

    Where to next?

    Glancing up, I saw an open window.

    The footsteps came nearer.

    No choice, I thought. Up I go.
```

Notice how the only difference between the two examples is where I broke them into paragraphs. Short paragraphs are easy to skim and consume. Long paragraphs feel bulky and slow your reader down.

Both of these are valid techniques, but understand the effect each one has on your reader. If you want your reader to slow down, use long paragraphs. For a fast read, shorter paragraphs feel more urgent.

3. Vary paragraph length

Most writers know to vary their sentence lengths to make paragraphs more interesting. On the other hand, many forget to vary their paragraph length.

A one-sentence paragraph between two longer ones makes a bigger impact, especially if you can summarize the impact in a few words.

Short paragraphs work.

See how simple the above paragraph is? This technique can be effective in improving the impact of stories, persuasive essays, or even just a letter to a friend. Summarize your point in as few words as possible, and surround it with text that explains it further.

Simple concept. Big impact.

These tips will help you write more engaging material for your readers. Experiment with these ideas, and see how they can help you write more effectively.

I've never taken drugs, but I want to write about someone who does

First, congratulations on never taking drugs. Please keep it that way!

And if you have taken or are taking drugs, consider stopping. It's not worth it.

A lot of beginning writers think they have to experience something in order to write about it. I've seen too many young writers who feel that they have to "suffer for their art".

This is a mistake.

Let me be perfectly clear: **never** use your writing as an excuse to damage yourself.

You don't have to commit a murder to write a mystery.

You don't have to suck blood to write about a vampire.

You don't have to chop off an arm to write about someone who loses a limb.

You don't have to experience something dangerous in order to understand it. Drugs, alcohol, and cutting are inexcusable. If you're tempted to do any of these things, please seek counseling or talk with a trusted adult. This is a symptom of a dangerous problem.

For example, if you're interested in learning about drug abuse, here's what you should do if you want to learn enough to add some realism to your writing:

- Read interviews with former drug addicts online
- Contact drug abuse hotlines (make sure they're local and/or toll-free) and ask for information
- Visit websites that describe the effects of particular drugs (http://www.drugabuse.gov is a good resource)
- Read books written by other authors that focus on similar effects

When doing research, place your own safety first. No story is worth putting your own life at risk.

If you plan to meet a drug addict or convicted criminal in person, make sure that several trusted adults know (especially your parents). Just telling your friends is not enough. Let one of those trusted adults help you set up a safe environment, such as an interview at a prison that is overseen by guards or a phone call where the addict/convicted criminal does not have access to your number.

Another option might be to volunteer at a soup kitchen or homeless shelter. The leaders there should have procedures in place to help keep you safe.

You can use similar concepts when researching other risky topics, such as how to make Molotov cocktails to blow up zombies or watching YouTube videos about how to pick a lock.

Don't actually create things like Molotov cocktails yourself—you could seriously injure yourself, and it's illegal in many areas (or at least regulated). If you're going to try it, make sure that you enlist the help of an explosives expert who understands how to do so safely.

There's a misconception that many authors are alcoholics or drug addicts. It is true that some well-known writers struggled with alcoholism or drug addiction, including Stephen King and Ernest Hemingway.

Stephen King later overcame his addiction and continues to write bestsellers. On the other hand, Hemingway eventually committed suicide. These people might have been successful writers (in the financial sense), but were not happy with their lives while under the influence of drugs and alcohol.

While these writers are enjoyed by millions of readers, they could have been better. Without drugs and alcohol clouding their mind, many of these writers may have gone on to write even greater stories.

Real writers are creative, not self-destructive. Be a real writer.

WHO'S AFRAID OF THE BIG BLANK PAGE?

NOT ME, NOT ME, NOT ME!

FAQs

"He who asks a question is a fool for five minutes;
he who does not ask a question remains a fool forever."

— Chinese proverb

How do I get started writing?

A good first step is to read this book and perform the exercises. It's okay if your story isn't perfect at first. They never are. In my opinion, it's best to generate a few story beginnings and then focus on your favorite.

If you're looking for more examples of writing prompts, consider checking out *Writing Advice for Teens: Writing Prompts*.

I have a cool book idea. Should I find a publisher?

Sorry, but no. At least not right away. In almost all cases, you have to write the story first.

After you've written your story, you'll have to edit to make it as perfect as you can. For some initial tips on editing your own work, check out the next book in this series: *Writing Advice for Teens: Editing.*

Also, if you're pursuing traditional publishing, you shouldn't go directly to the publisher. In most cases, you'll want to find a literary agent. Agents understand the publishing world, and they will help you get the best deal for your completed book.

For some non-fiction books, you can sometimes find an agent or publisher before writing the book. Even in that case, you'll still have to write something called a "book proposal", which is usually twenty or more pages long. The contents of a book proposal are beyond the scope of this guide, but usually include a summary of the project, an outline, a market analysis, and some sample chapters. You'll also need credentials: something that makes you uniquely qualified to write the book.

For fiction, you almost always find an agent or publisher *after* you've written your novel, not before. Once you've written one novel, a publisher may ask you to write additional novels as part of a multi-book deal, but you will still need to write that first book to get to that point.

You can find more tips on the publishing process in *Writing Advice for Teens: Preparing for Publishing.*

What's the difference between writing and publishing?

Writing is what happens when you actively work on creating a story. This creation process is the focus of this book.

Publishing is the process of making your story available for the world to read. This should only be attempted when your story is as perfect as possible.

How do I deal with writer's block?

See the section titled: *Typical Writing Problems* on page 121.

How do I become a better writer?

The short answer: practice.

The long answer: practice a lot.

It's going to take work. Take writing classes, read books on writing, and above all else, write. The more often you write, and the more often you edit your own work, the better you'll become.

Join a critique group. Writing can be lonely, and the support you get from the other people in your group will help motivate you. Also, finding problems in other people's work will help you identify issues within your own stories. Plus, you'll also learn by fixing the problems that your group members discover in your work.

Which other writing books should I read?

Of course, I'd love it if you read the rest of the books in the *Writing Advice for Teens* series.

Check out the *References* at the back of this book for a list of other great resources. There are lots of good books out there, and the ones listed are those I found most useful.

How long should my story be?

Most full-length novels tend to be between 80,000 and 100,000 words. For more details and examples of popular novel word counts, see *Appendix A: Word Count Guidelines*.

How do I make my story longer?

From time to time, I am asked for general strategies to make a manuscript or short story longer.

The writers who ask this question generally aren't looking to merely increase the word count of their manuscript, but instead feel like their story is missing something. However, these writers aren't sure how to coax the additional details from their story.

The best option is to use a critique group to help find holes in your story that need a little more explanation or development. That's not always possible, so there are a few things you can do on your own.

Reread your story with your readers in mind. As a reader, what am I likely to find interesting? Are there opportunities for adding a bit more backstory to help your readers understand why a particular character makes a specific decision?

Examine your plot. Is there any missing time? How does a reader know what's happened in between scenes? Are there opportunities to increase tension and conflict?

Consider your characters. Is there an interesting character you'd like to spend more time with? Go ahead and do so…after all, it's your story.

Sometimes your story has just come to its natural end. If you feel that you've done all you can to improve your story, it may be time to submit your manuscript to an editing service or a set of early, or beta, readers to get their take on the story.

Keep in mind that editing services will cost money, while beta readers will usually help you in exchange for a free copy of the book. If a beta reader happens to be a writer, she might also ask you to return the favor one day.

Editing services or beta readers can often help you find holes in your plot or identify opportunities to further explore an interesting character or concept.

A literary agent or publisher may also make suggestions to change your manuscript so that it will sell better in the marketplace. This may result in lengthening or shortening your story.

Avoid adding "fluff" to make your word counts. It's going to unnecessarily slow your story down, and you'll just end up having to edit it out later. Writing is hard enough on its own—don't make it harder.

How do I choose names for my characters, creatures, or settings?

Choosing names can be tough. On the other hand, they're also one of the easiest things in your story to change. As William Shakespeare said in *Romeo and Juliet*: "A rose by any other name would smell as sweet." What matters is the *essence* of the character, not what he or she is called.

That said, the right name can help your reader remember physical details. For characters, if they exist in our world, use names that reflect the heritage of the main character. Nicknames can also be used to reflect a character's personality or appearance, like Cobra, Tiny, or Shadow.

Let's say that we are thinking of writing about a red-headed girl. What do we call her, without knowing anything else? Red hair indicates an Irish heritage, so Rachel, Kate or Shannon would work well, among many others. You can search through baby naming websites for ideas, and you can often search based on country names.

When you've selected a name, write a little bit about the main character. See if you feel like the name fits. For example, let's try this example of a mother and her two young children:

```
Rebecca laughed, her auburn hair
shimmering in the sun. Her green eyes
twinkled.

Shane, her toddler, had just popped a
bubble. He stared at his hands expectantly,
shocked that the beautiful object had
disappeared.

His eyes welled up with tears, but then
Emma, his older sister, blew more bubbles
through her wand. Shane's face lit up as he
giggled at the wondrous world of bubbles
suddenly around him.
```

Here I've introduced three characters, but focused on each one a bit differently. As you write, I recommend that you use the first name that comes to mind. You can always change it later.

For naming creatures (beyond your normal pet names or everyday animals), there are two main strategies:

- If the story takes place in our world, use existing legends about faeries, ogres, and other mythical creatures.
- If the story takes place on an alien world or a spaceship, you can use mythology (like Greek or Norse) or scrambling words (like using Neila instead of Alien).

Places can be named in a similar fashion. For another option, consider the culture of the setting you'd like to create. If the inhabitants speak in a rough and guttural language (like ogres or trolls), look at German or Russian names for inspiration. Alternatively, if the inhabitants speak in a smooth and flowing language (like elves or faeries), you might look at the romance languages (French, Spanish, Italian) for inspiration.

Let's tackle a more unusual example: creating a new name for a disease.

Exercise: A new disease

Diseases are often named after the doctor who discovered them. Look for a last name in a phonebook that looks interesting, and use that. Perhaps you'll call it Smythe's Syndrome, or Johnson's Disease. Have fun with it.

If you find a name that looks close, but the name seems too normal, try changing the spelling to make it more interesting. That's what I did with "Smith" in "Smythe's Syndrome".

Afterward:

Create symptoms for your fictional disease. Do victims get warts that ooze puss? Does their hair fall out? What kind of disease might a teenage mastermind want to unleash on his school as revenge for all those years of being teased as a geek?

How do I choose a point of view?

As stated in the section on *Story Construction*, the two most common perspectives are first person and third-person limited. Ask yourself whether you'd rather tell the story directly to the reader (using "I", or first-person narrative), or if you'd prefer to use character names to show the story (third-person limited narrative)

If you plan to write comments addressed directly to the reader (like this!), I'd recommend a first-person narrative. If you prefer to keep the reader in the story, third-person limited is usually better.

Age and genre also make a difference. Younger readers prefer first-person narrative because it's easier to identify the main character. First-person narrative is also used when the reader should find out details at the same time as the main character, such as mysteries. Fantasy and science fiction is generally written in third person, as are most books for adult readers. These are just trends, not hard-and-fast rules. Do what's right for your story.

In any case, just make your best guess for a first draft. *Writing Advice for Teens: Editing* discusses how to fix common perspective problems.

Is it okay to mix perspectives?

There are two ways to interpret this question:

1. Is it okay to use both first-person and third-person perspectives within the same story?

In general, no.

If you use a first-person narrative, stick with just what the main character knows. If you want the reader to know what another character is doing, the main character should find it out at the same time as the reader.

As writers, we often want our readers to know everything that's happening within the story. However, most readers will get confused when reading a story that suddenly shifts from first-person to third-person narrative. If you shift perspectives this way, make sure to only do it at a chapter break.

In all of my stories, my number one goal is to avoid confusing the reader. The reader should always understand exactly what's happening, even if they don't know why (at least not yet). Making big shifts at chapter breaks helps avoid confusion because the reader expects something to change.

There may be an author who has used a shift from first- to third-person successfully, but I haven't seen a book that does this well. Until you have more experience, I recommend sticking with what's worked well for other authors, which means sticking with either first-person or third-person narrative, not mixing the two.

2. Is it okay to have multiple point-of-view (POV) characters within the same story?

Yes, that's usually okay, as long as you're using a third-person perspective. Always choose the characters who best tell your story. Use the smallest number of POV characters that makes sense for your story.

Some readers prefer sticking with one character all the way through, while others enjoy following multiple characters. This is a reader's preference, and unfortunately there's not much you can do about that.

One pitfall to avoid is changing the perspective too often. When critique partners read your story listen for the key phrase "this feels like it jumps around". This is a hint that your book is changing perspectives too often.

Authors who have used multiple POVs successfully include: J.R.R. Tolkien (the *Lord of the Rings* series), George R. R. Martin (*A Song of Ice and Fire* series), and Ann Brashares (*Sisterhood of the Traveling Pants*).

How do I make my dialogue sound realistic?

The best advice I can give here is to listen to others. Go to the mall, sit on a bench, and eavesdrop on people as they walk by. Watch movies. Pay attention to your own conversations with friends.

After you've taken some notes, think about your characters. Do they sound like someone you know or an actor in a movie? Listen to how they speak, and mimic the patterns in your stories.

You'll also want to make sure there's legitimate give-and-take. For example, avoid "leading questions" like this:

> "How was school today?"
>
> "Fine."
>
> "Did you meet any girls today?"

> "Yes, one."
>
> "What was her name?"
>
> "Amber."
>
> "Amber who?"
>
> "Amber Lombeck."
>
> "What is she like?"

And so on. Notice how every other line is a question? It's really boring to read a bunch of dialogue like this. Consider this next example, where there's more interaction between the characters.

> "How was school today?"
>
> "Fine. I met a cute girl."
>
> "Oh, really? Who's that?"
>
> "Amber. Amber Lombeck. Can I borrow the car tonight? We're supposed to go out for dinner."
>
> "Sure, here are the keys. What is she like?"

Even though we don't really know who's speaking, you probably get the sense that it's a parent/teenager relationship, where the teen is comfortable enough to discuss a potential girlfriend.

Once you've written the dialogue, read it out loud. Ask friends to act out the parts, only reading what's actually spoken. Ask yourself if the words reflect how people really talk. Adjust your dialogue until it sounds like a real conversation.

How do I know when my story is finished?

Let's be honest: no writer really knows for sure.

If you've just finished the first draft, your story is not ready. You definitely need to edit—not just proofreading for typos and grammar, but also for whether your story makes sense. See *Writing Advice for Teens: Editing* for more advice on editing your story.

You can gain confidence that your story is ready through critiques from other writers, but there's always something you can improve.

Another strategy is to put your manuscript away for a few months and edit again before you decide to query agents. Eventually, most writers decide that a story is "good enough" and move on to the next.

You'll never please every reader, so you should keep that in mind. Always aim to please yourself first.

Ideally, you need a few things to ensure that your work is ready to pursue publication:

- Confirmation from experienced writers or editors that the overall story seems solid
- Feedback from several (if not all) beta readers that they liked the story
- Ensure your work is free from typos.

Your final draft may be much different than your first draft, especially if you're just getting started as a writer. That's okay (and expected). Consider your own feelings too—never publish something if you'd be embarrassed to see your name on the cover.

If you've self-published a story and it's getting lots of 1- or 2-star reviews (and very few 4- or 5-star reviews), pull it down. That's evidence that your story wasn't ready for release. You don't want to ruin your reputation by keeping it up.

With a traditionally-published book, you may not have this option because the publisher is in control. On the other hand, with a traditionally published book, editors should be able to help you avoid issues that result in many 1- or 2-star reviews.

How should I handle criticism?

Writers need to develop an iron skin. There are going to be people who like what you write, and others who don't. You'll never please everyone.

Even *Harry Potter and the Sorcerer's Stone*, one of the best-liked books I know, with over 4,800 5-star reviews at the time of this writing, also has over 80 1-star reviews.

There's a difference between critiques and criticism. Critiques focus on the writing. Criticism, however unfairly, often focuses on the writer. In general, ignore criticism, as hard as that might be. Personal attacks are never okay.

Examples of bad criticism:

- You suck!
- My dog could write a better book.
- Don't quit your day job.

Examples of good critiques:

- The story felt a little slow when Ben and Angela were talking about their puppy. I wanted to skim through that part. Consider shortening or deleting it.
- There were a lot of typos in this submission. Please use spellcheck next time!
- I thought Amber fell in love with Jason too quickly. As the reader, I don't understand why she'd like a guy who seems like such a jerk. Give me some hints that explain why she likes him despite his faults.

Notice the big difference between bad criticism and good critiques: the criticism focuses on the writer, while the critique points out what was wrong and gives a suggestion on how to fix it.

Even when a critique focuses on the work, it can hurt to see your work torn apart by another writer. In my writing groups and editing business, submitted pages are often filled with red ink as I point out concepts I like and areas that need work. When my critique partners review my submissions, my work is covered in red ink too. No one is immune.

If you see red ink on your story after spending hours, days, weeks or even longer writing it, you may feel like you wasted your time.

You didn't. If you hadn't submitted anything, no one could have critiqued you. You would have learned nothing.

When your work is critiqued, learn from the suggestions. Are you consistently making the same mistakes? Are readers confused at the beginning of each chapter because you always start with dialogue? Do you often forget to incorporate sounds into your setting? Check for those things yourself before your next submission.

Let's say that a certain piece of feedback upsets you. For example, let's say that you get the following comment from a critique partner:

```
As I read this, I was left wondering why
Ellie would fall in love with John. He
seems like a bully, and I don't understand
what she sees in him.
```

Your immediate response might be something like:

```
Well, obviously John's cute, and he also
helped Ellie distribute Thanksgiving dinner
at the local food pantry. Of course most
readers will get this. That's dumb
feedback.
```

Always thank the submitter for their comments, regardless of how you feel. It's also okay to say "I'll think about it" and move on. Remember that you are the author, and if you disagree with the feedback, you're free to disregard it.

In any case, set aside any comments you disagree with and come back to them in a week. After calming down and removing emotion from the equation, you might find that the submitter made a valid point. You might end up thinking something like:

```
Well, it's true that John's cute, and I
covered that pretty well in the section
where Ellie falls in love with him. From
the reader's perspective, though, there are
fifty pages between the Thanksgiving dinner
```

```
at the food shelf and where she first
thinks she likes him. Maybe that's too
distant for the reader. I should add some
more details about her thoughts just before
she wants to kiss him.
```

For the above example, recognize that you need to give the reader reasons to understand why your characters fall in love.

If one person thinks that something is a problem, see if others agree. If two people make the same comment, pay attention—there might really be something you need to change. If three people point out the same issue, it's a real problem. Fix it.

Feedback is helpful even when it results in more work for the writer. Thank your submitter for taking the time to help you improve.

I just discovered a book/game/movie with the same plot. What should I do?

Don't get discouraged just because an idea has been done before. You can always improve on a past idea or take it in different direction.

One teen writer I mentored found himself in a quandary: he'd been working on a story for a year, and discovered that a recently announced game took place in the same location and involved the same historical figures. He asked me whether he should abandon his work and start on something new.

My response:

"Is the plot different? As long as the plot is different, you should be fine."

Yes, there may be some critics who will think he was influenced by the game, but if his story is unique, he shouldn't have a major problem. All of the characters, locations, and time periods are historical, so they're fair game for use in a story.

He might even turn the historical similarities into an advantage: people who enjoyed the game may also enjoy his book. This gives him access to a market of people who have already shown interest in the area.

If the plots are too close, then someone might think he created a derivative work. A publisher who accepts your novel will have a legal team who will excel at looking into issues like this. If you've already done the majority of the work, you may as well try submitting it.

Even if this teen writer had decided not to go forward with his project, he should still feel encouraged. Someone else obviously thought that the time period, location, and historical figures had commercial appeal, so it shows he had good instincts when he began his story.

What about fan fiction?

Fan fiction is a term that describes stories written by fans that borrow characters and settings from existing works.

These stories are fine to write for fun, but never try to sell or profit from them. Unless the work is in the public domain, like William Shakespeare's plays, the original stories are protected by copyright.

Fan fiction is considered a "derivative work", or a story directly inspired by the original story. Under U.S. law, you can't publish these stories because it infringes on the original copyright.

Some authors, like JK Rowling, encourage fan fiction because they believe it helps inspire the next generation of writers. On the other hand, there are many others who will legally pursue those who post fan fiction.

If you choose to write fan fiction, do it for fun, not for profit. Be aware that if you post fan fiction on the Internet, it's likely that the copyright owner will eventually ask for the website to take it back down.

How do I make my story unique?

Making your story unique is a definite challenge. Be careful, though—just tossing a purple bunny into your story probably won't be enough. "Unique" does not necessarily mean "strange".

Instead of creating unnecessary new creatures, focus on creating likeable characters and interesting situations. Once your readers start rooting for your main character, they'll quickly forget about whether the story is unique enough.

Also, bring in your own unique experiences. Sure, most readers know what it's like to fall in love, but how many people fall in love while walking their dog? Most readers know what it's like to go to school, but how many find out their teacher is actually a zombie?

Many situations have happened before. What makes your story different? In most cases, it's your own thoughts and experiences that make your story unique.

What if someone tries to steal my idea?

Realistically, unless you're already a famous author, most people aren't going to be interested in stealing your story.

There's also a difference between the idea behind a story (zombies infecting each other through a disease) and the story itself (*Dawn of the Dead, I am Legend, Zombieland,* etc.). Story ideas can't be protected, but the stories themselves are protected by copyright. The exact protections offered will vary by country, but in the US, a story is protected by copyright the moment you write it down. See *Writing Advice for Teens: Preparing for Publishing* for more details on copyright.

Unfortunately, if someone else uses the same story concept, there's nothing you can do to stop them. What you *can* do is write your own best possible version of the story. Ultimately, it's the story itself that sells, not the base concept.

To protect your story, only provide copies to people you trust. Even this isn't always enough—Stephanie Meyer distributed a few electronic copies of a draft of her fifth book in the *Twilight* series to trusted friends, and one of them uploaded it to a file-sharing site. While she doesn't believe that the person acted maliciously, she still decided to stop all work on that book. So far, she hasn't started again.

The best way to ensure your story is protected is to only provide it to other writers. Since you'll likely be reviewing their work as well, other writers are unlikely to steal your work. It's also best to avoid sending full manuscripts unless you already have a pre-existing relationship. Start with a couple chapters, and eventually you'll learn which people you can trust.

If you're really concerned about someone stealing your work, you can introduce a few intentional typos or word differences so you can track which manuscript was stolen. For example, you might replace a few "he said" phrases with "he exclaimed". Subtle changes like this are unlikely to get noticed, but will help you identify a stolen copy.

For what it's worth, I've been writing for over a decade and never had someone steal my work to present it as their own. As a general policy, I do keep track of all of my development (printouts, old emails, etc.) to prove that I developed the concept. However, I've never had to use this proof, and with luck, never will.

Parting Thoughts

*"We are all apprentices in a craft where
no one ever becomes a master."*

— *Ernest Hemingway*

Writing takes work, but that's what makes it rewarding and enjoyable. Every day that you spend writing is another day where you'll learn something new and improve your craft.

There will be days where writing feels hard.

Keep trying.

Don't give up.

Success will take practice, and it will take dedication.

Each day you write is another day where you might be writing the next bestseller. You never know when inspiration will strike. Even so, by writing every day, you increase the chance of capturing those wonderful ideas.

As you skim over the final pages of this book, consider sharing some of the tools you've learned with other writers. Gone are the days where writers work alone—we now need other writers to help us succeed and spread the word about our stories. By helping others, you'll build relationships that will last you a lifetime.

Stop putting off your goals. Get a little bit closer, even if it's only a few more words.

Get started.

Write now.

Mike Kalmbach

ARE YOU WRITING YET?

APPENDIX A:
WORD COUNT GUIDELINES

When talking with other writers, know the right term for the type of story you're writing. The following guidelines are not absolutes, but are commonly accepted ranges for different story lengths.

- Micro-Fiction: 1 - 100 words
- Flash Fiction: 100 - 1,000 words
- Short Story: 1,000 - 7,500 words
- Novellette: 7,500 - 20,000 words
- Novella: 20,000 - 50,000 words
- Novel: 50,000 - 110,000 words

Within each story genre, the rules vary. Here are several common genres with suggested word counts. Especially for a first novel, aim for the middle of the range.

- Picture Books: 200-500 words
- Early Readers: 500-2000 words
- Chapter Books: 5,000-10,000 words
- Middle Grade: 25,000-45,000 words
- Young adult: 55,000-90,000 words
  - YA fantasy, sci-fi, and paranormal tend to be longer: 70,000-90,000 words
  - Everything else will vary
- Adult: 70,000-115,000 words
  - Romance: 85,000-100,000 words
  - Mysteries, Horror, Crime: 75,000-95,000 words
  - Sci-fi and Fantasy: 80,000-120,000 words
  - Literary and Women's Fiction: 80,000-100,000 words

To help give you an idea of the size of typical books and their word counts, here are several examples of the word counts of several popular books. For simplicity, all word counts are rounded to the nearest thousand.

Anne Frank: The Diary of a Young Girl by Anne Frank – 83,000
Breaking Dawn by Stephanie Meyer – 188,000
Catching Fire by Suzanne Collins – 102,000
Charlie and the Chocolate Factory by Roald Dahl -31,000
Eclipse by Stephanie Meyer – 148,000
Ender's Game by Orson Scott Card – 101,000
Harry Potter and the Sorcerer's Stone by J.K. Rowling – 77,000
Harry Potter and the Chamber of Secrets by J.K. Rowling – 85,000
Harry Potter and the Prisoner of Azkaban by J.K. Rowling - 107,000
Harry Potter and the Goblet of Fire by J.K. Rowling – 191,000
Harry Potter and the Order of the Phoenix by J.K. Rowling – 257,000
Harry Potter and the Half-Blood Prince by J.K. Rowling – 169,000
Harry Potter and the Deathly Hallows by J.K. Rowling – 198,000
Little Women by Louisa May Alcott – 184,000
Lord of the Flies by William Golding – 60,000
Moby Dick by Herman Melville – 206,000
Mockingjay by Suzanne Collins – 100,000
My Sister's Keeper by Jodi Picoult – 120,000
New Moon by Stephanie Meyer – 133,000
Old Yeller by Fred Gipson – 36,000
The Caldarian Conflict by Mike Kalmbach – 98,000
The Fellowship of the Ring by J.R.R. Tolkien – 177,000
The Golden Compass by Philip Pullman – 113,000
The Hobbit by J.R.R. Tolkien – 95,000
The Hunger Games by Suzanne Collins – 100,000
The Lion, The Witch and the Wardrobe by C.S. Lewis – 36,000
The Mouse and the Motorcycle by Beverly Cleary – 22,000
The Outsiders by S.E. Hinton – 49,000
The Return of the King by J.R.R. Tolkien – 134,000
The Secret Garden by Frances Hodgson Burnett – 80,000
The Two Towers by J.R.R. Tolkien – 143,000
Twilight by Stephanie Meyer – 118,000
Treasure Island by Robert Louis Stevenson – 67,000
To Kill a Mockingbird by Harper Lee – 99,000

APPENDIX B:
EXAMPLE CHARACTER SHEET

A printable version is downloadable from
http://writingadviceforteens.com/character_sheets.

> Character photo or drawing here

Story/Series Name:

Character name:

Character Information (only fill in applicable fields)

Personal Information

Nickname(s): _____   Does s/he like it? _____

Full Name: _____

Meaning of Character's Name: _____

Type of housing: Apartment / Condominium / Small house / Medium house / Large house / Mansion

Lives in: _____
                City   State   Country

Communication methods: Letters / Landline / Cell phone / Email

Birth Date: _____   Marital Status: Single / Married / Divorced   Gender: M / F

Physical Appearance

Age: _____   Does s/he look older or younger? _____

Hair color: _____   Straight / wavy / curly / bald

Eye color: _____   Glasses / Contacts

Weight: _____   Height: _____   Thin / Normal / Obese

Skin tone: _____   Scars: _____

Piercings: _____   Tattoos: _____

Physical activity: Near-Death / Couch potato / Average shape / Athlete / Superhuman

Dominant hand: Left / Right   Wears jewelry? (specify type) _____

Typical clothing style: _____

Cologne / Perfume: _____

Health Information (if applicable)

General health condition: Excellent / Good / Normal / Poor / Terminally ill

If unhealthy, why? _____

Disabilities: _____

Superpowers: _____

Medications: _____

Allergies: _____

Fears: _____

Mental Health: _____

Personal beliefs (if applicable)

Religious beliefs: _____

Active in religion?   Yes / No   Describe: _____

Active in politics?   Yes / No   Describe: _____

Is family important? Describe: _____

Is money important? Describe: _____

Optimist / Pragmatic / Pessimist   Introvert / Extrovert

Believes in ghosts?   Yes / No   Believes in UFOs?   Yes / No

Believes in magic?   Yes / No   Believes in conspiracy theories?   Yes / No

Background Information (if applicable)

Hometown: _____   Rural / Suburban / Urban

What was childhood like? _____
Earliest
memory: _____

Most important life event: _____

How did this affect him/her? _____

Highest level of education: None / Elementary / Middle School / High School /
                                 Associates / Bachelors / Masters / Ph.D.

Favorite subject(s): _____

Most classmates would call this character: Popular / Nerd / Jock / Freak / Average / Bully

What happens the week before the story starts? _____

Personality / Goals (if applicable)

Basic strategy for solving problems: Brute strength / Speed / Accuracy / Avoidance / Moral high ground / Personal gain

Biggest priority: _____

Likes him/herself?   Yes / No   Describe: _____

Strengths: _____

Weaknesses: _____

Are weaknesses apparent to others?   Yes / No   How does s/he hide it? _____

Most embarrassing memory: _____

Biggest regret: _____

Deepest, darkest secret: _____

If granted one wish, it would be: _____

Lifelong goal (s): _____

Mannerisms: _____

Favorite sayings: _____

Romantic relationships (if applicable)

Ever been in love?   Yes / No   What happened? _____

Believe in love at first sight?   Yes / No   Experienced it?   Yes / No

Ever cheated on someone?   Yes / No   Ever been cheated on?   Yes / No

Attracted to: Blondes / Brunettes / Redheads / Grey Hair   Men / Woman

Most desired traits: Intelligence / Athletic / Social / Adventurous / Quiet
Describe romantic
experience: _____

Relationships with others (if applicable)

Best friend(s): _____

Worst enemies: _____

How is s/he perceived by co-workers? _____

How is s/he perceived by friends? _____

How is s/he perceived by family? _____

What do others like **most** about him/her? _____

What do others like **least** about him/her? _____

Family Relationships (if applicable)

Mother's name: _____ Alive / Dead   Get along / Always argue

Father's name: _____ Alive / Dead   Get along / Always argue

Stepmom's name: _____ Alive / Dead   Get along / Always argue

Stepfather's name: _____ Alive / Dead   Get along / Always argue

Spouse's name _____ Alive / Dead   Get along / Always argue

Siblings: _____

Children: _____

Extended family: _____

Pets: _____

Special notes
about family
relationships: _____

Job / Financial Information (if applicable)

Employer: _____

Job Title: _____

How long has this character held this job? _____ Salary: $ _____

Spending habits: Frugal / Average / Spends everything   Cash / Check / Credit Card

Likes / Dislikes (if applicable)

Favorite color: _____   Least favorite color: _____

Favorite music: _____   Least favorite music: _____

Favorite movie: _____   Least favorite movie: _____

Favorite TV show: _____   Least favorite TV show: _____

Favorite food: _____   Least favorite food _____

Favorite book: _____   Least favorite book: _____

Favorite holiday: _____   Least favorite holiday: _____

Likes sports?   Yes / No   Favorite team(s): _____

Hobbies: _____

Plays these musical instruments: _____

Speaks these languages: _____

Usually spends Saturday night: Home alone / Intimate dinner / At a party

GLOSSARY

Antagonist: The character, creature, machine, or natural force that prevents the protagonist from accomplishing his goal.

Atmosphere: Used in regards to Setting, see Tone.

Autobiography: A story of the author's life, written in his own words.

Beta readers: Those who read an early version of a manuscript and provide feedback that will be incorporated into the final draft. These readers are typically fans of the genre and are not necessarily writers.

Character: A person as used within a story.

Character arc: A phrase that describes how a character changes throughout the course of a story.

Character triangle: A technique used by authors to create tension through the conflicting desires of three different characters.

Cliché: An overused phrase, e.g., fit as a fiddle.

Cliffhanger: A method used to end a chapter at a moment of tension. This often compels a reader to turn the next page or look forward to the next story.

Climax: The point where the major conflict within a story is resolved.

Clips: A publishing term used to describe articles previously published under an author's name.

Conflict: The tension between a character's goal and the events that prevent him from reaching it.

Criticism: Typically negative, criticism points out problems within a work. It may focus on the writer instead of the work. Good writers give critiques instead of criticism.

Critique: A constructive method of finding problems within a work, while also pointing out areas that are done well. Often, potential solutions are presented with the problems.

Critique partners: Fellow writers who help each other find and eliminate problems from stories.

Derivative work: A story that is directly inspired from a pre-existing work. Fan fiction is a common type of derivative work. Never attempt to sell a derivative work without permission from the copyright holder of the original creation.

Dialogue: A conversational exchange between characters within a story.

Dialogue fingerprint: A phrase used to describe the manner in which a character speaks. Each character should have phrasing, vocabulary, or a verbal tic that makes him or her unique.

Dialogue tags: Descriptive terms that indicate who is speaking or convey emotion behind a conversation, such as "said", "asked", or "snarled".

Draft: A version of a manuscript.

Editing: See Revising

Ending: The conclusion of a story.

External conflict: Outside forces that the main character struggles against, such as other characters, nature, and society.

Falling Action: The segment of a story between the climax and ending. This typically diffuses the tension within a story.

Feedback: Reactions to a work that may include both positive and negative aspects.

Foreshadowing: Subtle hints of forthcoming events within a story.

Genre: A classification of stories that contain similar elements, such as romance, mystery, or science fiction.

Hook: A method of drawing a reader's interest with the story's opening.

Information dump: Giving the reader too many details at one time.

Introduction: The story's opening. This section introduces the reader to the characters, setting, and underlying plot.

Internal conflict: A struggle within a main character's mind, such as overcoming addiction or making a hard decision.

Internal editor: The voice in your mind that criticizes your work as you write. While needed during revisions, this voice should be ignored while you're writing the first draft.

Mood: See Tone

Moral: The basic lesson of a story.

Narrative: The words used to tell a story to a reader.

Outline: A high-level description of the events within a story.

Overwriting: Including too much detail within a story. This often leads to information dump.

Perspective: The method used within the narrative that tells the reader who is telling the story. See the *Story Construction* section to learn more.

Plot: The sequence of events within a story.

Plot arc: A phrase that describes how tension is affected by the sequence of events within a story.

Plot twist: A surprise event that changes the direction of a story. This is commonly used to maintain a reader's interest in a story.

Point-of-view: See Perspective

Prose: Ordinary language used in the written word with no intentional rhythm or rhyme. See also *Narrative*.

Protagonist: The main character, or hero/heroine of a story.

Query letters: A letter used to introduce an agent or publisher to a manuscript or article.

Quotas: A goal used to define how much work a writer should complete each day.

Raising the stakes: A method used to make a main character more directly involved in the outcome of a sequence of events. This typically increases the tension within a story.

Revising: The process of improving a manuscript.

Revision: See Draft

Rising Action: The segment of a story between the introduction and the climax. This is a sequence of events that increases the overall tension of a story.

Rule of Three: A writing strategy used to improve a story's effectiveness, humor, and satisfaction. This may also help improve a story's flow.

Self-publishing: A process by which an author makes a manuscript available to readers without going through an established publisher. The author handles all costs and aspects of the process, including cover design, editing, and marketing.

Setting: The location where a story takes place.

Show: A method of conveying a character's emotions through her actions. For example, if a character smiles, this typically conveys happiness. This is generally preferred over Telling.

Subplot: A set of events that add interest to a story but is not central to the main conflict. For example, a mystery story may include elements of romance.

Tell: Directly conveying a character's emotions to a reader. For example, saying "I am happy" tells the reader exactly how the character feels.

Tone: Describes how a story makes a reader feel. A tone might be scary, suspenseful, or friendly.

Traditional publishing: A process where an author offers a manuscript to an established publisher. The publisher handles all aspects of cover design, editing, and marketing in exchange for a majority of the proceeds. The author typically receives a cut of all sales.

Transformative climaxes: The main character is notably changed by the moment of peak tension within a story.

Twist: See Plot twist

World building: A method of sprinkling setting details throughout a story's events. The details should resonate within a reader's mind to create a vivid world.

Writer's block: A phrase that describes the frustration writers experience when they don't know what to write.

WRITER (NOUN):
1. SOMEONE DRIVEN TO CREATE
2. ONE WITH A DESIRE TO SHARE.
3. SOMEONE LIKE YOU.

REFERENCES

There are several more books planned for this series. Watch for updates at http://writingadviceforteens.com.

The next book in this series:
Writing Advice for Teens: Editing
Expected September 2012

Coming soon:
Writing Advice for Teens: Joining the Writing Community
Writing Advice for Teens: Preparing for Publishing
Writing Advice for Teens: Writing as a Career
Writing Advice for Teens: Writing Prompts

Within this book, I mention several times that writers must read. I've found the following resources to be invaluable in helping shape my own writing career. Consider adding them to your reading list.

- *20 Master Plots* by Ronald B. Tobias
- *45 Master Characters* by Victoria Lynn Schmidt
- *Book in a Month* by Victoria Lynn Schmidt
- *Characters & Viewpoint* by Orson Scott Card
- *Hooked* by Les Edgerton
- *Make a Scene* by Jordan E. Rosenfeld
- *Manual of Style* by the University of Chicago Press Staff
- *On Writing* by Stephen King
- *On Writing Well* by William Zinsser
- *Plot & Structure* by James Scott Bell
- *Story Engineering* by Larry Brooks
- *The Breakout Novelist* by Donald Maass
- *The Element Encyclopedia of Ghosts & Hauntings* by Theresa Cheung

- *The Element Encyclopedia of Secret Societies* by John Michael Greer
- *The Elements of Style* by William Strunk Jr. and E.B. White
- *The Fire in Fiction* by Donald Maass
- *The Nighttime Novelist* by Joseph Bates
- *The Story Within* by Laura Oliver
- *The Tipping Point* by Malcolm Gladwell
- *The Weekend Novelist Re-Writes the Novel* by Robert. J. Ray
- *The Writer's Digest Guide to Query Letters* by Wendy Burt-Thomas
- *The Writer's Little Helper* by James V. Smith, Jr.
- *Write to the Point* by Rosemary T. Fruehling and N.B. Oldham
- *Writer with a Day Job* by Aine Greaney
- *Writing Down the Bones* by Natalie Goldberg
- *Writing the Breakout Novel* by Donald Maass

INDEX

Agents, 139
Airplane, 122
Alcohol, 136
Antagonists, 108, 163
Back to the Future, 90
Becoming a better writer, 140
Beta readers, 163
Brainstorm, 131
Brand names, 96
Breaking the rules, 133
Breaks, 42
Bunnicula, 89
Character arcs, 91, 163
Character sheets, 87
Character triangles, 89
Characters, 25, 84, 163
    choosing names, 142
    flaws, 90
    goals, 89
    main, 84
    major, 84
    minor, 84
    reactions, 91
    weakness, 90
Children's books, 24
Cliché, 106, 163
Cliffhanger, 163
Climax, 110, 163
Clips, 163
Conflict, 91, 104, 163
    external, 104
    internal, 104
Copyright, 153

Creativity, 43
Criticism, 149, 164
Critique, 164
Critique group, 140, *See* Writing group
Critique partners, 164
Dawn of the Dead, 153
Dedicated writing time, 58
Derivative work, 164
Dialogue, 89, 146, 164
Dialogue tags, 88, 164
Discovery writing, 115
Distractions, 38
Doubt, 20
Draft, 164
Dreams, 20
Drugs, 135
Editing, 164
Encouragement
    You can make it as a writer, 13
Ending, 113, 118, 119, 164
Examples
    Cliffhanger, 19
    coke, 96
    computer crash, 129
    Faeries, 77
    first-person narrative, 92
    Fish taste good, 124
    Humor, 26, 27
    Introducing characters, 85
    One-sentence prompt responses, 67

outline, 116
pop, 96
Prompt matrix response, 69
Publish short stories (monthly plan), 51
rivalry, 46
Scene outline, 40
second-person narrative, 93
setting, 99
soda, 96
Still life, 76
Teenagers, 89
third-person limited narrative, 94
third-person omniscient narrative, 94
Writing a novel (monthly plan), 45
Exercises
A bright sunny day, 102
A new disease, 144
Cliffhanger, 20
Current events, 73
Diseases, 79
History prompts, 70
Journal entry, 34
Map out your plan (outline), 119
Meet your main character, 87
My distractions, 37
Old dog, new trick!, 78
One-sentence prompt, 68
Prompt matrix, 70
Secrets in the attic, 66
Still life, 75
Tell a joke, 28

The mystery door, 65
The plot thickens, 114
What do you enjoy?, 23
Why write?, 17
Your first month's schedule, 56
Exercising, 125
Falling action, 112, 164
Feedback, 30
First draft, 17, 37, 50
Focus, 35, 39, 41, 132
Foreshadowing, 164
Genre, 164
Getting started, 139
Goal. *See* Word count
Growth, 35
Harry Potter, 48, 55, 90, 111, 149, 158
Hook, 20, 106, 165
Humor, 26, 123
I am Legend, 153
Information dump, 99
Into the Land of Iowah, 88
Introduction, 105, 165
Jack and the Beanstalk, 106
Journal. *See* Writer's journal
Juno, 106
Making stories longer, 141
Master in Fine Arts, 14
Molotov cocktails, 137
Mood, 40
Nanny McPhee, 106
Narrative, 165
Outline, 40, 115
Overwriting, 86
Paragraph lengths, 133

Perspective, 92, 144, 145, 165
  first-person, 92, 145
  second-person, 93
  third-person, 93, 145, 146
Plot, 25, 102, 151
Plot arc, 102, 165
Plot twist, 113, 165
Point-of-view. *See* Perspective
Precautions
  backups, 83, 128
Prioritize, 131
Procrastination, 123, 125
Protagonists, 108, 165
Publisher, 139
Publishing, 140
Quotas, 166
Raising the stakes, 109, 166
Rejection, 55
Relaxation, 43, 121, 122
Respect
  for fellow writers, 30
Revising, 166
Revision, 166
Rising action, 108, 166
Roanoke, 70
Rule of three, 24
Scenes, 39, 58
Self-publishing, 166
Setting, 25, 95, 166
  choosing names, 143
Showing, 100, 166
Stephanie Meyer, 153
Sticky notes, 128
Stress, 42
Subplot, 112, 166

Tasks, 130
Tell, 166
Telling, 100
Text message, 128
The Caldarian Conflict, 40, 95, 158
The Fellowship of the Ring, 106, 158
The Magic Thread, 91
tone, 101
Tools, 60
  Grindstone, 62
  LitLift, 61
  Scrivener, 61
  Write or Die!, 62
Track progress, 57, 59, *See also* Writer's journal
Traditional publishing, 167
Twilight, 153, 158
Twist, 167
Vampires, 79, 80, 81
Voice mail, 127
Voice recorder, 126
Word count, 28, 32, 37, 39, 48, 49, 57, 157
World War II, 72
Writer's block, 65, 121
Writer's journal, 32, 57
Writing, 140
Writing goals, 43
  long-term, 43
  monthly, 44
  plans, 44
  SMART (mnemonic), 44
Writing group, 29, 41
Writing routine, 31
Zombieland, 153
Zombies, 137

DID YOU ENJOY THIS BOOK?

Help the author.

Tell your friends.

Post your review on:

Amazon
BN.com
Goodreads

Like his author page at:

http://www.facebook.com/mikekalmbachauthor

To find out more about Mike and his upcoming projects, please visit:

http://mikekalmbach.com

ABOUT THE AUTHOR

Mike Kalmbach has a Master of Science degree in software engineering from the University of Minnesota. Moonlighting as a freelance editor, he has edited numerous full-length manuscripts as well as countless shorter works.

He also leads the Rochester MN Writing Group and is a founding member of the Rochester Writers Collaborative. He is a strong believer in the power of community, and has led online writing groups and forums for over ten years. Mike enjoys writing for his blog and interacting on Twitter.

Mike currently lives in the Rochester, MN area with his wife Brenda, his son Alex, and their two cats.

Find out more about Mike at:

http://mikekalmbach.com
http://twitter.com/mikekalmbach
http://www.goodreads.com/mikekalmbach
http://www.facebook.com/mikekalmbachauthor

CPSIA information can be obtained at www.ICGtesting.com
Printed in the USA
LVOW121542020513

332035LV00014B/494/P

9 780984 654536